D0975046

Tree

A LIFE STORY

DAVID SUZUKI &

WAYNE GRADY

Art by ROBERT BATEMAN

Tree

A LIFE STORY

David
Suzuki
Foundation

GREYSTONE BOOKS
DOUGLAS & MCINTYRE PUBLISHING GROUP
VANCOUVER / TORONTO / BERKELEY

Greystone Books
A division of Douglas & McIntyre Ltd.
2323 Quebec Street, Suite 201
Vancouver, British Columbia
Canada V5T 4S7
www.greystonebooks.com

David Suzuki Foundation
2211 West 4th Avenue, Suite 219
Vancouver, British Columbia
Canada V6K 4S2

Library and Archives Canada Cataloguing in Publication
Suzuki, David, 1936–
Tree : a life story / David Suzuki and Wayne Grady; art by Robert Bateman.
Includes bibliographical references and index.

ISBN 1-55365-016-6

1. Douglas fir—Life cycles. 2. Douglas fir—Development. 3. Douglas fir—Growth.
I. Grady, Wayne II. Bateman, Robert, 1930– III. Title.
QK494.5.P66S88 2004   585'.2   C2004-903383-2

Library of Congress information is available upon request

Editing by Nancy Flight
Copyediting by Naomi Pauls
Jacket and text design by Jessica Sullivan
Jacket art by Robert Bateman
Printed in Canada by Friesens
Distributed in the U.S. by Publishers Group West

Greystone Books is committed to reducing the consumption of old-growth forests
in the books it publishes. This book is one step toward that goal. It is printed on acid-free paper
that is 100% ancient-forest free, and it has been processed chlorine free.

We gratefully acknowledge the financial support of the Canada Council for the Arts,
the British Columbia Arts Council, and the Government of Canada through the Book Publishing
Industry Development Program (BPIDP) for our publishing activities.

This book is dedicated to Ellen Adams,
whom I first met as a graduate student in zoology
at the University of British Columbia.
She was bright and vivacious
and had interests far beyond the field of zoology.
She died too young. In her generosity,
she supported the work of the David Suzuki
Foundation and has helped to make this book possible.

DAVID SUZUKI

CONTENTS

ACKNOWLEDGMENTS

A book is like a single tree in a forest, in that it exists in conjunction with and because of a great many others around it. Our thanks to the many biologists and researchers who have studied Douglas-fir and who brought its amazing characteristics to light. Our thanks also to Rob Sanders, at Greystone Books, who enthusiastically and relentlessly hounded us to complete the manuscript.

To Nancy Flight, who gave the original text her usual perceptive reading and excellent guidance, and to Naomi Pauls, whose copy-editing skills saved us from many embarrassments, we extend our deep gratitude. We also want to thank Alex Gabriel, who did a superb job of gathering research material for the book. It is an honor to have the wonderful art of Robert Bateman in our book.

Friends who have helped in many ways with the preparation of this book include Karen Landman, Chris Pollock, Larry Scanlan, Genni Gunn, Frank Hook, Elois Yaxley, and Faisel Moola.

INTRODUCTION

This book is a biography of one tree, a Douglas-fir, but it could be any tree—an Australian eucalpytus, an Indian banyan, an English oak, an African baobab, a mahogany from the Amazon, or a cedar of Lebanon. All trees attest to the wonder of evolution, the ability of life to adapt to unexpected challenges and to perpetuate itself over vast periods of time.

Rooted securely in the earth, trees reach toward the heavens. All across the planet, trees—in a wonderful profusion of form and function—literally hold the world together. Their leaves receive the Sun's energy for the benefit of all terrestrial creatures and transpire torrents of water vapor into the atmosphere. Their branches and trunks provide shelter, food, and habitat for mammals, birds, amphibians, insects, and other plants. And their roots anchor the mysterious underworld of rock and soil. Trees are among Earth's longest-lived organisms; their lives span periods of time that extend far beyond our existence, experience, and memory. Trees are remarkable beings. Yet they stand like extras in life's drama, always there as backdrops to the ever-changing action around them, so familiar and omnipresent that we barely take notice of them.

I am a zoologist by choice and training. All my life, animals have commanded my attention and my passion. The very first animals I became aware of were my parents, siblings, and playmates, followed by my dog, Sport. My parents were avid gardeners, but plants never excited me; they were not cute and did not move or make sounds. Fishing was my childhood passion, salamanders and frogs were prized catches in expeditions to ditches and swamps, and the amazing variety of insects, especially beetles, was a constant fascination. It was not an accident that I spent my adult career as a geneticist studying an insect, the fruit fly *Drosophila melanogaster*.

So why would an animal lover write a book about trees? Ever since Rachel Carson's seminal book, *Silent Spring,* focused the world's attention on the importance of the environment, people have decried the destruction of the world's forests and the unsustainability of industrial-scale forestry practices. Like many activists, I have been swept up in the movement to protect old-growth forests in North and South America, Asia, and Australia but have mainly been concerned about the habitat they provide for other organisms, the loss of biodiversity in such forests, and their role in global warming. It was a single tree near my island cottage that finally moved me to realize what a marvel a tree is.

A trail winds from my cottage to the beach, sloping steeply where the soil ends and the sand begins. There, at the soil's edge, a magnificent Douglas-fir towers over 50 meters (160 feet) tall and perhaps 5 meters (16 feet) in circumference. It may be four hundred years old, which means it began its life around the time Shakespeare began writing *King Lear*. It is a peculiar tree because it juts out horizontally from the bank above the beach, then arcs upward at a 30° angle, and finally turns straight up. The horizontal section of the trunk is a wonderful place to sit or begin to climb, and we have hung ropes around the rising trunk to suspend swings and hammocks.

That tree has endured our activities, provided shade, fed squirrels and chipmunks, and harbored eagles and ravens, but it always hovered on the periphery of our consciousness. One day, I lazily gazed at the misshapen trunk of that tree and realized with a shock that hundreds of years ago, when it was just starting to grow—say, about the time Isaac Newton observed an apple falling from a tree in England—the land on which the tree first germinated must have slumped toward the beach, tilting the tree out on an angle over the sand. The young stem had to alter its growth pattern to keep climbing upward to the light. Years later, another slide of the land must have dropped the tree trunk further so that it was horizontal, while the upward curve had to compensate yet again to become vertical. That tree was mute evidence of history.

Any tree's life is precarious. A tree doesn't move; yet it must cast its pollen as far from its own territory as possible and then disperse its seeds into its own sphere of influence. It has evolved amazing mechanisms to achieve this, from exploiting animals as agents of dispersal to attaching propellers, parachutes, and catapults to a seed's tough casing. Anyone who has seen the mist of pollen above an evergreen forest, the gauzy clouds of cottonwood catkins along a quiet stream bank, or the piles of acorns during an oak's mast year knows the extravagant profligacy of trees to ensure survival of a very few. Wherever a seed lands, its fate is sealed, and for most that means lying exposed to predation by insects, birds, or mammals, withering on rock, or drowning in water. Even when a seed lands on soil, its future is in doubt. That tiny drop of protoplasm contains the entire legacy from its parent, a store of provisions to get it through its first tentative stirrings, and a genetic blueprint informing the growing plant to send its root down and its stem up and telling it how to capture the energy, water, and materials it needs to live. Its life is programmed; yet it must also be flexible enough to handle unexpected storms, drought, fire, and predators.

Once its first root punctures the soil, the seed is committed to that place on the planet and that is where it must derive everything it needs to survive and flourish for centuries. From the air and the soil, it must obtain all the elements required to make the molecules and structures that will allow it to tower tens or even hundreds of meters above the ground, weigh tens of tonnes, and be able to withstand the destructive forces of fire and wind. Human ingenuity and technology could never match the strength and resilience that are built into every tree. With only sunlight, carbon dioxide, water, nitrogen, and a few trace elements, a tree manufactures the entire spectrum of complex molecules that are the building blocks of its physical structure and metabolism. To accomplish this feat,

Douglas-fir at my cottage

trees have recruited the aid of fungi, which envelop the tree's roots and root hairs like a gossamer filigree, extracting trace elements and water from the soil, which are then exchanged with the tree for sugars made in its leaves.

A tree's protoplasm is packed with energy reserves and other molecules that are irresistible to other organisms. Trees cannot run or hide or swat attacking predators, but they are not helpless victims. Their bark behaves like a coat of armor, and they make a variety of potent compounds that act as toxins or repellents to invaders. If attacked by insects, trees can produce volatile compounds that not only repel the insects but also warn neighboring trees of the danger and stimulate them to synthesize the repellent. Trees provide room and board for fungi in their cells; in return, the guest produces substances that ward off bacterial infection. If overwhelmed by disease or pests, a tree may seal off the affected area, sacrificing limbs and other body parts for the survival of the rest. In the soil, roots of the trees in a community may mingle and actually fuse, thereby allowing the trees to communicate, exchange materials, and help each other out. No tree is an island; it is a communal citizen and derives the same benefits from cooperation, sharing, and mutual effort that any living creature receives from participating in a fully functioning ecosystem.

Over time, even the toughest tree is relentlessly punctured, penetrated, infected, and weakened. The death of a tree is not signaled by a still heart, flatlining brain, or final breath. A dying tree continues to function in fits and starts; roots attempt to send nourishment and water back through clogged and broken pipes; photosynthesis carries on in a spotty way. But eventually the tree becomes a lifeless snag, which nevertheless supports a huge number of other species. When it finally falls, the decaying tree continues to feed and support a succession of life-forms for centuries.

Throughout history, we have pondered our relationship with the rest of life on Earth. In the past, many peoples understood that we shared a dependence on and kinship with not only all other animals but all green beings. They imagined how the universe originated, when and why humans arose, and the way things came to be. The stories recounted in every culture embodied the observations, insights, and conjectures that make up each people's worldview.

Science represents a radically different and powerful way of looking at the world. By focusing on a part of nature, controlling everything impinging on it, and measuring and describing a particular fragment, we acquire profound insights—into that fragment. In the process, scientists lose sight of the context within which that part exists, no longer seeing the rhythms, cycles, and patterns that made the fragment interesting in the first place. Science's insights are in a steady state of flux, constantly being amplified, altered, even displaced by fresh observations. In this book, we have tried to restore a layperson's sense of wonder and questioning and added the kind of information acquired by scientists. The details will change and grow over time, but the phenomena remain as wonderful and dazzling as ever.

The story of a single tree connects us to other times and to all parts of the world. This book tells that story. But it is also the story of all trees—and all life—throughout this place called Earth.

David Suzuki
June 2004

B I R H

Trees warp time.
JOHN FOWLES, *The Tree*

A lightning bolt illuminates the sky, striking the highest point of the forested ridge. The fire does not start at the top, however, where the trees are young and strong, but slightly lower down, where over the years snags and fallen branches have accumulated to form a stack of dried kindling. One standing snag smolders for days, dropping live embers onto the rocky soil beneath it. The coals spread into the surrounding litter and ignite a ground fire, which enflames small twigs and dropped cones in its path. The fire licks up and tickles the lower dead branches of the living trees, quickly ascending the ladder of interlaced branches into the resinous middle story, where it burns with such fierce intensity that it consumes all the oxygen in the surrounding air and reaches a temperature well above the flash point of living wood. Then, like a suddenly opened damper in a firebox, a charge of fresh oxygen borne in by the opportune wind is whipped by atmospheric convection, and all the flames in the world seem instantly, as if by some devilish magic, to explode into the forest canopy. What started as a ground fire is now a crown fire, which is a fire on the move.

The crown fire advances by sending scouts ahead of it, looking for fresh resources. First the main fire begins to wave back and forth, as though uncertain of what to consume next; then its tendrils twist into little ringlets of flame, spirals and whorls and mini-tornadoes, which soon combine to form one huge, angry vortex, a whirling silo of rolling smoke. The gases at the top, burning at temperatures in the range of 1000°C (1800°F), are sucked down to the bottom, where they pick up burning branches and sometimes entire logs and carry them up the updraft enveloping the silo, which now acts as a cannon and fires them hundreds of meters into the unburned forest. The air is filled with flaming missiles. Their mission is to start spot fires, or satellite fires, which then merge before reporting back to the main fire.

When the space between the main fire and the united spot fires becomes hotter than the flash point of wood, and is fed by the wind with its burden of fresh oxygen, suddenly, in milliseconds, there is no distinction between the main fire and its colonizing scouts. This is called a blowup. A fire that has been slowly advancing suddenly occupies a hundred square kilometers (40 square miles). It no longer moves linearly; it is a spreading wildfire. The whole forest is a chaos of flame-laced smoke and searing heat, of animals and birds screeching and blundering in the dark, of loosened boulders and roaring winds and the seeming end of all living things.

When every last stick of flammable material in the area has been consumed, when the ground has been stripped of vegetation and sterilized of organic nutrients, when even the water has evaporated from the creek beds, when the rocks have cracked and smoke and particulates from the fire's burning have spun up to the very limit of the Earth's atmosphere, the juggernaut of fire moves on, following fresh scouts to exploit new territory in whatever direction geography and the wind determine for it. What it leaves behind is silence. The hissing and the roaring have departed; there are no animals, no birds or reptiles or insects, no wind in the willows, no rattle or scrape of branch on branch. No movement. No color but charcoal and ash gray. A person looking upon such a desolated scene would be forgiven for thinking that fire is a scourge from the nether regions that Dante, writing halfway across the world around the time that our fire erupted, called the Inferno. Rain comes from heaven; fire comes from hell.

SUCH A PERSON would be wrong. The west coast of North America, where this fire took place, has experienced such conflagrations regularly. The really huge fires, the century fires, swept through the northern forests every two hundred to three hundred years; smaller ground fires blazed as often as twice every three decades. Since the big trees, the mature Douglas-firs, the Sitka spruces, and the giant sequoias, live for more than a thousand years, it follows that they are not consumed by even the biggest fires. In fact, big trees depend on big fires to advance and complete their life cycles.

The great fires come from neither heaven nor hell. They are part of the natural processes that govern the life of plants and animals. Fire is energy that originated in the immense cauldron of nuclear fusion that is our Sun. Solar energy streamed down on Earth and was captured by leaves and then transferred into stable molecules that are regularly, if accidentally, reignited and transformed back into fire. This century fire is as much a part of the life of the forest as rain, or the hum of insects or the chirr of northern flying squirrels and red tree voles.

Lodgepole pines, giant sequoias, and other western conifers are serotinous, or late opening; instead of dropping their seeds as soon as they are ripe, as apple and maple trees do, they hang on to them and drop them in response to some environmental trigger. Lodgepole pines may keep their cones closed for fifty years, waiting for a fire to come along to open the cones and release the seeds. Sequoias also keep their cones tightly shut for decades, releasing the seeds only when the cones are heated to 50 to 60°C (120 to 140°F), and such temperatures can only be achieved by fire. Plant (and animal) tissue begins to break down at 50°C (120°F), which means these giants release their seeds at temperatures high enough to kill them. It is thought that the lowest branches on some conifers die and remain attached to the tree for no other purpose than to act as fuel to send ground fires shooting up into their crowns to heat the cones and spring the seeds.

The ability to withstand intense heat is a valuable attribute in areas with what is called a fire climate—low annual rainfall (less than 125 centimeters, or 50 inches, a year) with long, hot, dry

After the fire

periods and strong winds. Australia has such a climate, and its characteristic eucalyptus, or gum, tree is one of the most flammable trees on Earth, producing large quantities of dry leaves and even a flammable gas that can shoot flames a distance of 100 meters (300 feet). Yet gum trees can withstand incredible temperatures, and some species even seem to need fire to remain alive. Even in relatively moist climates, fire resistance can be an asset. In Hawaii, for example, the ohia lehua tree (*Metrosideros macropus*) can actually be buried alive under a pile of burning cinders from a volcano and still send out fresh shoots—it will even produce new roots under its pile of fresh ash.

Douglas-firs (*Pseudotsuga menziesii*) do not need fire to reproduce, but they do depend on fire for their survival. Their seedlings do not tolerate shade; the trees rely on fire to clear the ground around the bases of such lower-growing species as western hemlock and western redcedar so that when their seeds do fall, they will settle on untenanted, and therefore unshaded, terrain. Furthermore, ash contains precious nutrients upon which young seedlings can flourish. Without fire, Douglas-fir forests would eventually climax to hemlock and redcedar forests. Mature Douglas-firs can withstand these cleansing fires because they have evolved thick, nonflammable bark—up to 30 centimeters (12 inches) thick in mature trees—that protects the living cambium layer within.

Fire is whimsical. It can sweep through thousands of hectares of timber in a few days, seemingly bent on destroying everything in its path, yet leave a sapling here, a mature tree there, an entire stand of trees somewhere else. After this particular fire, a hasty glance across the blackened, burned-out valley might take in nothing but charred spires leaning above mounds of gray ash. But a closer look, especially after a rain, would reveal an occasional slash of green, a glint of sunlight from streaks of running resin, and in a sheltered spot on the downwind side of a low ridge, a small oasis of spared forest.

Although Douglas-fir cones do not require high temperatures to prise them open, they must be dried to less than 50 percent of their natural moisture content. Within days of the conflagration, the hundreds of pendant cones on a single, defiant, 70-meter (230-foot) Douglas-fir slowly spread their scales and release their store of winged seeds to the unimpeded wind. The seeds whirl and spin their way to the ground. Ninety-five percent of them will never germinate, falling on rock, into water, or onto barren soil. Ninety-five percent of the rest will die within their first year, from lack of nutrients, too much shade, or the appetites of enterprising deer mice or Douglas squirrels. But nature's extravagance ensures that a few—enough—will land on moist, mineral soil that will stimulate germination. Most of those will never achieve maturity, falling victim to another fire before they are sufficiently barked, a browsing black-tailed deer, an elk using them for a too-vigorous antler rub, insects, fungal disease, drought, a landslide, a killing frost, or competition from other trees. But one of them will establish itself in a clear, high, well-drained spot, with plenty of sunlight and a steady, moisture-laden breeze rising from the Pacific Ocean at the sparkling end of the regreening valley. The seed will send out roots, grow a stem, sprout branches, spread needles, and continue to mature for the next 500 years or so. It will be our tree.

IN THE *B*EGINNING

Fire is a familiar and essential component of forest ecosystems; fires reduce matter and energy from the forest's life-forms to their basic components, which can be reexploited by new life-forms.

Fire, seed, and the subsequent growth of our tree are stages in a process that began eons before there was animal life on Earth. Our universe was fired in the kiln of the Big Bang 13.8 billion years ago, when all existing matter was compressed into a singularity, a point no larger than the period at the end of this sentence. The point then exploded with unimaginable force, temperature, and speed, spewing outward in an expansion that continues to this day. For the next 9 billion years, eddies of cooling gas contained enough matter to exert a gravitational pull that drew the gases into ever-denser clots. Suddenly, on the cosmic time scale, the heavens were illuminated by the near-synchronous ignition of billions of nuclear furnaces—the stars. One of them was our own star, the Sun, created from a cloud mass that comprised more than 99.8 percent of all matter in its solar system.

The planets formed from condensation of the 0.2 percent of universal gaseous matter that was not tied up in the Sun. As Earth coalesced, around 4.5 billion years ago, the local gravitational pressure squeezing it together heated its core into magma. The planet's atmosphere, oxygenless but laden with such greenhouse gases as carbon dioxide and water vapor, formed an insulating blanket that trapped the Earth's heat and stabilized its surface temperatures at a level compatible with life. Thus, the stage was set and the lights turned on for the great drama of life about to be performed.

These are the opening scenes: Earth's surface cooled into immense plates of solid crust, which floated on the magma like gigantic ice floes on a sea of molten fire; where they collided, they thrust skyward, creating mountain ranges, and where they pulled apart, oceans rushed in to fill the gaps. All the while—a while being more than half a billion years—the hydrologic cycle of evaporation, condensation, and precipitation established itself on the barren land, etching it with canyons as torrents flowed, dissolving minerals from the rock that washed into the seas, where over millennia they accumulated and joined with elements already present in water. The oceans became a rich solution of carbon, nitrogen, phosphorus, sulfur, hydrogen, and sodium. The land acquired a thin dusting of sand, gravel, volcanic ash, silt, and clay.

Around the middle of Act 1, these building blocks combined in the oceans to form living organisms. How they did so is one of the most fiercely debated questions in modern biology, but most agree that it happened sometime around 3.8 or 3.9 billion years ago, in water, in a process that required energy. That energy may have come from a variety of sources: ultraviolet rays from the ozoneless atmosphere, lightning, meteorite showers (which, according to some hypotheses, also carried in a few essential elements missing from the Earth's mix), and hydrothermal vents on the ocean floor, where magma oozed up from cracks between the tectonic plates, superheating the water and providing such ingredients as methane and ammonia.

A few atoms and molecules eventually accreted into larger aggregates, macromolecules of lipids, carbohydrates, proteins, and nucleic acids. Somehow, complex molecules came to be enclosed by lipid membranes that separated the in from the out. These were protocells, the beginning of life. At some point, lifeless matter had become arranged in sufficient complexity to become alive. End of Act 1.

Today life is distinguished from nonlife by a number of properties, none unique to living organisms but collectively exhibited only in living creatures—highly ordered structures, reproduction, growth and development, utilization of energy, response to the environment, homeostasis (maintenance of an internal environment), and evolutionary adaptation. We have no idea how many potential life-forms flickered into existence only to succumb to pressure from other potential life-forms, environmental conditions, or a lack of resources or resourcefulness, and disappear back into unformed matter. It may be that, given the richness of molecular substrates in the primeval oceans, spontaneous aggregation happened all the time. If so, competiton must have been ferocious and the price of failure ruthless. Only one experiment proved successful. Once a life-form appeared that could outcompete all others, reproduce itself, and mutate in ways that increased its competitive edge, that single protocell of a bacterium became the progenitor of all future life on Earth, the last instance on the planet of spontaneous generation of life from nonliving matter. After that, only life begat life, in an unbroken line to the present.

Life at the beginning of Act 2—the first few hundred million years—was not easy. Early bacterial cells had to scrounge for a living in the ocean, using energy liberated by broken sulfur bonds between atoms, for example, to carry out chemical reactions, or huddling about deep-sea hydrothermal vents for warmth. Much of this minimal activity might have taken place under several kilometers of ice, as Snowball Earth went through successive phases of severe cooling. For tens of millions of years, those early life-forms evolved, shaped by the changing environment and by natural selection.

The basic engine of evolution is mutation: rare and unpredictable variations in an organism's genetic blueprint. For a few generations, all of an organism's genes are reproduced according to plan as an organism simply divides into two by binary fission.

But then suddenly and randomly, in one offspring, a gene is inherited that is altered, different, a mutant. In the early years after life arose, mutations were opportunities, generating variations that might confer a slight advantage.

Today, after billions of years of evolution, any living organism is the recipient of a genome that has been honed over eons of natural selection. Like the parts in a finely crafted watch, painstakingly developed by generations of Swiss watchmakers, genes in a nucleus have been selected to function properly during an organism's life. If we were to remove the back of the watch and blindly plunge a needle into the mechanisms, there is a finite chance that such a random event might improve the functioning of the watch, but chances are overwhelmingly high that the action would have deleterious consequences. An event causing a mutation can be thought of as analogous to the needle in the watch, which is why most mutations are detrimental, making the offspring less fit for survival in its parental habitat. But once in a long while a mutation accidentally confers an advantage: a slight, almost imperceptible increase in the efficiency of a metabolic reaction, for example, or the unaccountable enlargement of an appendage that, when wriggled, provides propulsion. The advantaged offspring survives and outcompetes the rest of its siblings, and evolution occurs. Still, waiting for mutations to occur is an arbitrary and slow way to advance life.

Evolution sped up considerably, however, with the invention of sex. Sexual reproduction beats the other kind hands down. Sex leads to genetic mixing and shuffling to generate massive numbers of new combinations, greatly increasing the probability of a genetic mix conferring a slight advantage. And, coincidentally, introducing the necessity of death. When a cell reproduces without sex, as all life did over the early millions of years, by simply growing and dividing into two, both daughter cells are identical to each other and to the parental cell that gave birth to them. All three cells, parent and the two daughters, have the same chance of surviving, provided the habitat remains unchanged. Each cell is essentially immortal, since it can go on splitting into two indefinitely. When there are two parents, however, the number of possible outcomes increases exponentially, which means that many more different gene combinations are produced than can survive.

Let's say that each parent is carrying two forms, or alleles, of the gene a; one parent is carrying two a^1 genes, and the other parent is carrying two a^2 genes. Through sexual reproduction and genetic shuffling, there will be three possible combinations in later generations: a^1a^1, a^1a^2, and a^2a^2. Now suppose that a different gene, b, also exists in two states: b^1 and b^2. Now the number of possible combinations rises to nine: $a^1a^1b^1b^1$, $a^1a^1b^2b^2$, $a^1a^1b^1b^2$, $a^1a^2b^1b^1$, $a^1a^2b^1b^2$, $a^1a^2b^2b^2$, $a^2a^2b^1b^1$, $a^2a^2b^1b^2$, and $a^2a^2b^2b^2$. If there are three genes with two forms, the number of combinations jumps to twenty-seven. If there are n genes, the number of combinations is 3^n (that is, 3×3 n times). And that is assuming only two forms of each gene, whereas in reality, there may be dozens of different forms of each gene, thereby ramping up even further the number of possible combinations. The recent decoding of the entire human genome suggests that we each carry perhaps as many as 30,000 genes, which means if there were only two forms of each gene, the number of genetic combinations would be $3^{30,000}$, a number beyond comprehension. With such huge variation, competition exploded and many of those cells had to die. The introduction of sex was the biological bite into the forbidden fruit that caused life on Earth to be expelled from the Garden of Eden.

For nearly 2 billion years, single-celled bacteria were the only life that existed on the planet. Were we to travel back to that time, Earth would appear lifeless to the naked eye, since cells are only visible with the magnification of microscopes. But the oceans teemed with a cornucopia of different life-forms, all competing for resources and a place to use them. It was a microbial planet. In many ways, it still is. Today, scientists find ancient bacteria existing 15 kilometers (9 miles) below Earth's surface, embedded in solid rock. There they eke out an existence, breaking chemical bonds for the energy holding atoms together, slurping up water molecules in the rock, and dividing, perhaps as little as once every one to ten millennia. Locked in the rocks, those bacteria were freed from the vagaries of ice ages and warm periods, continental drift, and huge changes in flora and fauna. They are like museums, preserving genetic conditions that may be billions of years old. Incredibly, living bacteria have been found in the fossilized gut of a 40-million-year-old bee. It is estimated that the weight of all the planet's microbes exceeds that of all multicellular creatures, from trees to whales to grass to human beings. And as we shall see, we are all, humans and trees alike, elaborations of those original bacterial strategies for survival.

But then the plot took a twist. During a warm cycle, an organism resembling modern cyanobacteria (blue-green algae) found a way to photosynthesize—to capture a few of the vast streams of photons of sunlight raining on the oceans' surface and to use that energy to transform them into sugar that could be stored and called forth as needed. These photosynthesizers, the first organisms on Earth that could be called plants, spread throughout the oceans 3.5 billion years ago, filling up the top 200 meters (650 feet). They were so good at exploiting the energy flooding Earth's surface that other, nonphotosynthesizing bacteria offered their own protoplasm as shelter for the photosynthesizers in return for some of the sugars.

This ancient cooperation for mutual benefit was so successful that associations for other functions, such as cell division and energy production, developed in similar symbiotic relationships. Protected and nourished within their borrowed protoplasm, the photosynthesizing cells eventually tied their entire future to their hosts' cells by becoming totally integrated and dependent organelles called chloroplasts. Photosynthesis was the chemical process that made almost all of the vast array of independent, self-reproducing life on this planet possible, and its benefits were shared through cooperation among cells. There were also side benefits: the uptake of carbon dioxide reduced the amount of heat trapped above Earth's surface and released an interesting by-product—oxygen.

Initially, these photosynthesizers were bacteria, or single-celled organisms known as prokaryotes. Like all evolutionary "breakthroughs," the early models of photosynthesizers must have been crude, but compared with those that could not exploit sunlight, they still had a huge advantage. But again, as they spread, they began to compete, and through natural selection, photosynthesis became ever more efficient and diverse. Not all bacteria were photosynthetic, but those that were, freed from competing for energy sources, quickly took over the oceans. As phytoplankton, they still own the oceans today and account for more than half of all the photosynthesis that takes place on Earth; that is why they have been referred to as "the ocean's invisible forest."

Sometime between 3.5 and 2.5 billion years ago, one prokaryotic group split off from the rest to form three new lineages:

archaebacteria (the extremophiles, for example, which lived near or even in the deep-sea vents), eubacteria (continuing the line of photosynthetic cyanobacteria), and a third branch, which eventually became the eukaryotes, organisms with a nucleus. Each eukaryotic cell was an aggregate of originally mutualistic organisms that were so useful to the host that they became organelles such as chloroplasts and mitochondria. The first eukaryotes were single-celled organisms. They became the building blocks of multicellular organisms, the group that now comprises all animals and plants. Multicellularity enabled specializations of cells within an individual; a multicellular eukaryote is a colony of many different cell types, each of which carries out a task that benefits the collective, on the understanding that what benefits the collective benefits the cell. Cooperation, as demonstrated by both cellular organelles and multicellularity, is as much a driving force in nature as competition and confers a selective advantage in the ruthless game of natural selection.

Almost all of the 100 trillion cells that make up a human being are able to metabolize, grow, and divide by themselves, given the proper nutrients. Each is almost fully competent to qualify as an independent cell, and yet each is integrated within a larger whole. An individual human being is thus a colony of potentially self-sufficient cells that appeared at some point during evolution by cooperating for the greater well-being of the whole. And from this aggregate whole emerged human consciousness, a new property that is far more than the mere expression of the sum of all of the parts.

Right from the beginning, multicellularity was a curious blend of selfishness and altruism. Each cell was released from the burden of taking care of all the little household tasks that prevented it from doing any one of them really well. One group could concentrate on digestion, for example, while another could specialize in reproduction. A third could be devoted to energy acquisition, or photosynthesis, organizing itself onto a large surface—such as fronds—to absorb enough sunlight to supply the entire collective with energy and at the same time outcompete surrounding organisms for space in the Sun.

About 450 million years ago, most likely as a result of population density and extreme competition, some plants moved out of their marine environment onto land. Washed ashore by tides or blown onto land by massive storms, instead of dying, some organisms adapted to a challenging environment of limited water but also opportunities—sunlight that was not filtered out by water and an atmosphere that was rich in carbon dioxide. This was the end of Act 2.

As early plants spread across the land, they encountered plenty of sunlight, but in leaving the marine environment, they were no longer bathed in water containing dissolved minerals, elements, and small molecules. Carbon dioxide had to be extracted from air, and new ways had to be found to locate and absorb the nutrients, trace elements, and water needed for photosynthesis. On land there was dust, silt, sand, gravel, and clay, but no soil. Only after generations of terrestrial plants lived and died—their hard-won minerals and molecules added to the inert matrix covering rocks—was soil created, over hundreds of millennia. In a few million years, plants on land accounted for the other half of the photosynthesis taking place on Earth.

On land now covered with soil and reservoirs of water, in a landscape coated with plants, jockeying for a piece of the Sun intensified. In Darwinian terms, competition favored aggressiveness and innovation, the internecine struggle for survival. Individuals that found new ways to gain access to light survived by edging out their siblings that did not. Darwin called it "the great battle of life." Competition was most severe, Darwin wrote in *The Origin of Species*, "between allied forms, which fill nearly the same place in the economy of nature." In other words, the worst wars in nature are always civil wars, brother against sister, offspring against parent. Every advantage is pressed, every weakness exploited. "Each organic being . . . at some period of its life, during some season of the year, during each generation or at intervals, has to struggle for life and to suffer great destruction." In a field filled with the same species of plant, those that stood a little taller than the others were going to thrive at the expense of their siblings.

Sometime before the Carboniferous period, which began 235 million years ago, some individual descendants of the species that had invaded the land raised themselves tentatively above the ground, stole sunlight from their brethren, and prospered. To do this successfully without being blown over by winds or waves or pulled down by other plants struggling to imitate their success, they had to develop stiffness in their stems and firmness in their roots. They had to become trees.

A HOME IN THE *S*OIL

Although the seeds of some plants, such as the giant sequoia, prefer ash-laden soil, Douglas-fir seeds can lie dormant for years, waiting for nitrogen and other nutrients to be restored to the soil matrix. Nitrogen is essential for life; it is a constituent of nucleic acids and proteins and makes up 2 percent of our body weight. Nitrogen is abundant in air, making up 78 percent of it. But in soil it is found in only 5 parts per million; the low concentration of nitrogen is the biggest factor limiting plant growth. And on the steep slopes of the Pacific coastal mountains, incessant rain readily washes nutrients such as nitrogen out of the thin layer of soil. Because nitrogen is not a highly reactive element, it has to be converted by a living process to either ammonia or nitrogen oxide before it can be taken up and used by an organism. This conversion is called nitrogen fixation.

In the forest, nitrogen is removed from the air and fixed in the soil by bacteria such as *Clostridium butyricum*. This bacterium is destroyed at temperatures above 82°C (180°F), which is easily exceeded by fire at the surface, where dormant Douglas-fir seeds tend to lie. In his book *Forest Primeval*, Chris Maser traces the clandestine pathway by which *C. butyricum* is reintroduced into the upper soil layers after a fire.

Deep beneath the surface, truffles, the fruiting bodies of various forest fungi, survive the fire. The bacterium lives on the truffles' skin, along with spores of yeast. Deer mice (*Peromyscus maniculatus*), perhaps the most widespread rodent in North America, are generalists in their diets; they prefer seeds but will not spurn nuts, berries, insect eggs and larvae, or mushrooms. They make large caches of seeds—it was deer mouse caches of pine nuts in the American Southwest that harbored the deadly hantavirus that causes Four Corners Disease—which means they have a strong attachment to their home ranges and will move back into an area after being driven away from it by, say, a fire. Flame, however, destroys much of their usual food supply, including their seed caches. So, scurrying about at night, they dig up and gorge on truffles—not a bad life—all the while defecating fecal pellets loaded with undigested *C. butyricum*. "Thus," writes Maser, "the burned soil is reinoculated almost immediately by the small mammals of the forest that transport truffle spores, nitrogen-fixing bacteria, and yeast from the live forest."

"Almost immediately" might be an exaggeration, but not much of one. Deer mice and other small animals—the Pacific Northwest is home to the most diverse animal community in North America, and dozens of species of moles, voles, chipmunks, gophers, shrews, mice, and woodrats are associated with the Douglas-fir forest— busily transform sterile wood ash back into productive soil. One study found that four species in particular—Trowbridge's shrews, vagrant shrews, deer mice, and creeping voles—were most active in cleared or burned forest areas. But even with a small army of defecating insectivores and rodents, it can take fifty to a hundred years for forest trees to complete the process of regeneration after a big fire.

Deer mice also love to eat Douglas-fir seeds, which are large and full of stored nutrients, and they are unlikely to escape notice if they lie out in the open too long. Our seed is somewhat luckier. Smoke from the century fire has seeded the atmosphere with dust particles, which have formed the nuclei of water droplets, and within days of the conflagration rain pours into the valley, solubilizing much of the ash, which then percolates into the soil. The rain fills the streambed and tumbles thousands of seeds downslope away from the fire-damaged area. Many are washed out to sea, where they feed marine creatures as they break down. Ours, however, becomes caught in a small backwash where the stream makes a sudden meander around a tumble of fallen rock, eddies out onto the floodplain, and settles there when the flow of water in the streambed subsides. The rain not only washes the land but also clears the skies, and when the clouds disperse, out comes the Sun and dries up all the rain.

As Earth spins along its path around the Sun, the seasons change. Eventually the temperature drops and the rain turns to snow, for our seed lies at an elevation where snow is the dominant form of precipitation from November until early April. Snow fills the valley and covers the scarred remains of the forest. Only the standing spars are black now, and the bottoms of the delicate holes made by the feet of elk and white-tailed deer that wander quickly through en route to more rewarding pastures lower down.

THE FOREST PRIMEVAL

After the retreat of the glaciers, more than 50 percent of Earth's landmass was forested—whatever was not mountain, tundra, prairie, steppe, or desert was trees. The world's forests covered 125 million square kilometers (nearly 50 million square miles) and included tropical rain forests, temperate hardwood forests, and northern needle-leaf, or conifer, boreal forests. Earth was the green planet. Trees sucked greenhouse gases from the atmosphere and replaced them with life-giving oxygen. They contributed nutrients and nitrogen to the soil, making it suitable for agriculture. Without forests, animal life on Earth would almost certainly still be primarily marine. And yet because of human activity, very little of those ancient successional forests remain intact, and little is known about the species richness they harbored. What vertebrates, insects, plants, fungi, and microorganisms depend on old-growth stands for their existence? What happens to weather patterns, erosion, wind, and solar effects when pristine, complex forest communities are replaced by agriculture or even second- or third-growth bushlands? Studies in South America, Australia and New Zealand, Asia, and Europe are barely beginning to reveal the distinctive characteristics of the original forests and of the species that lived within them and nowhere else, but powerful modern technologies and the heavy demands of exploding human numbers, consumption, and a global economy are now extinguishing species before they are even discovered.

Before the arrival of Europeans in the Pacific Northwest, Douglas-fir forests covered more than 77 million hectares (19 million acres) of mountain and coastal habitat, from central British Columbia south to Mexico and from the Cascade Crest in the east south into the Willamette and Sacramento valleys, up and over the Coast Mountains, and almost reaching the Pacific coastline, where a thin sliver of Sitka spruce, western hemlock, and coast redwoods separated the Douglas-fir forest from the sea. It is a relatively young ecosystem. At the end of the Wisconsin Ice Age, about eleven thousand years ago, the climate switched from subarctic to temperate, pushing the great deciduous forests east and bringing mild, wet winters and dry summers to the West, a climate more suited to conifers. The first species to move in was lodgepole pine, which predominated for thousands of years, until the climate warmed sufficiently. Then Douglas-fir took over, dominating the landscape with their tall crowns, thick trunks, and compact needles, completely outstripping the other trees associated with their new habitat—western redcedar and western hemlock in the north; Pacific yew and grand fir in the lowlands and valleys; ponderosa, Sitka spruce, sugar pine, tan oak, and Pacific madrone, or arbutus, in the southern ranges. Together, these temperate rain forests support the greatest biomass per hectare of any ecosystem on Earth. All over the planet, trees developed different strategies to survive by exploiting the unique climatic, geographic, and ecological conditions they encountered.

Douglas-fir is a pioneer species, which means that it moves quickly and efficiently into an uninhabited area and colonizes it, preferably to the exclusion of other species, at least until the trees are tall enough to overshadow them. Then lesser, more shade-tolerant species can shelter under their boughs for a while. But Douglas-fir flourishes if every few years a good, cleansing fire comes along and clears away the deadwood and low brush at its base so that its seedlings can prosper. The irony is that the lower trees, the hemlocks and the redcedars and the true firs, are all settler species. They are down there patiently biding their time until the big king trees get too massive for their root systems and topple to the ground, and then they can take over the territory.

Nineteenth-century nature writer John Muir was the first botanist to describe the Douglas-fir. He called it Douglas spruce, however, underscoring a problem with the nomenclature. The Douglas-fir is not a fir or a spruce or a pine, as it has also been called. That is why Douglas-fir is hyphenated. The tree's scientific name, *Pseudotsuga menziesii*, doesn't help. *Pseudotsuga* means "false hemlock," and *Menziesii* is after Alexander Menzies, who was royal botanist on Captain George Vancouver's *Discovery* and who collected seedlings of the tree when the ship sailed up the west coast of North America.

To Muir, the Douglas-fir was "by far the most majestic spruce I ever beheld in any forest, and one of the largest and longest lived of the giants that flourish throughout the main pine belt." Although to his southern Californian sensibility the Oregon forest, where the Douglas-fir predominated, was too dense and dark, the Douglas-fir and sugar pine forest of the high Sierra, where the trees were far-

ther apart and "barely 20 percent of the forest floor was not in sunlight at noon," was very heaven. "This vigorous spruce," he wrote,
"is ever beautiful, welcoming the mountain winds and the snow as
well as the mellow summer light, and maintaining its youthful
freshness undiminished from century to century through a thousand storms." Before the coming of Europeans, the Douglas-fir
forests were forests primeval.

NO ONE KNOWS for certain how many human beings inhabited
North America before Europeans arrived, but archeological and
DNA evidence suggests that North America was densely populated, rich in history, and diverse in cultures long before Columbus built his first gibbet on the beach of Hispaniola. The current
estimate has up to 80 million people living here in the fourteenth
century, nearly as many as were in Europe at the time. A great
number of those people were living in the Pacific Northwest for
more or less the same reason that a great number of people live
there now; the climate was mild, the fishing was great, the forests
were richly endowed with animal and plant life, and the mountains buffered them from the cares and machinations of the rest of
the continent. Recent archeological evidence from coastal island
and cave sites, places that were not covered by glaciers during the
Ice Age, suggests that the ancestors of these people did not come
across the mountains after crossing the Bering land bridge as has
previously been supposed but arrived much earlier by boat, perhaps from the same Polynesian islands the aboriginal peoples of
Australia had come from. They came from the sea.

Around the time our seed was soaking in sunshine in its sheltered spot beside the spill of rocks and debris, the Aztec Empire
was building its capital city, Tenochtitlán, now known as Mexico

City. No such megalopolistic plans were afoot in the Pacific Northwest, but the population was far from scattered. The Coast Salish, the people inhabiting the low-lying area between northern Vancouver Island in the north and the Columbia River in the south, lived in small clan-villages of perhaps three hundred people each and depended on fishing salmon from the rivers, harvesting clams and oysters from the coastal waters, and trading—every village was also a commercial center. The villages were small, but there were a lot of them. Each consisted of about one hundred families. The Coast Salish used and respected trees, fashioning dugouts, longhouses, and grave monuments from western red-cedars, which were huge enough but easier to fall and softer to carve than Douglas-fir and, perhaps more important, grew right down to the shoreline. They even made their summer clothing from its bark, as did the Polynesians. Like people of every part of the world, the aboriginal coastal cultures drew on their observational acuity and found many uses for the trees of their territory. They used roots of spruce for baskets, cedar for mortuary poles, green alder boughs for smoking salmon, and spruce gum to cover wounds. These were people of the salmon-forest.

Washington Irving, who wrote of the Coast Salish in 1836—shortly after contact—reports that "they had an idea of a benevolent and omnipotent spirit, creator of all things. They represent him as assuming various shapes at pleasure, but generally that of an immense bird." When this bird became angry, lightning flashed from its eyes and thunder clapped from its wings. They also spoke of a secondary deity, associated with fire, of whom they were especially fearful.

The "immense bird" was Raven. Raven was a kind of flying Coyote, a Trickster, a shape-shifter. Raven existed, in the words of Haida storyteller and artist Bill Reid and poet and translator Robert Bringhurst, "before there was anything, before the great flood had covered the earth and receded, before the animals walked the earth or the trees covered the land or the birds flew between the trees." Raven stole light and gave it to the firmament. He stole salmon from the Beaver and gave them to the rivers that ran down to the sea. And after the Great Flood subsided he found, lying in the sand encased in a gigantic clamshell, a horde of tiny, two-legged, featherless, beakless creatures. He croaked at them and they came scurrying out of their shell, blinking in the unaccustomed light. They were the first humans.

There is an ancient Babylonian story about Raven and the Flood. The Babylonian Noah, Uta-Napishtim, built an ark when the Great Flood came, and when he wanted to know if the waters had subsided he sent out a dove to search for land. The dove, finding no place to alight, came back to the ark. After a while Uta-Napishtim sent out a swallow. The swallow also found no land and came back. Then Uta-Napishtim brought out a raven and let it go free. The raven flew away and did not come back.

Now we know why. Raven landed on a beach in the Pacific Northwest and was busy coaxing the first human beings out of their clamshell. The first people of the West Coast, who had come from the sea.

THE *S*EED'S SURROUNDINGS

When the snow begins to melt, the soil under our seed warms and life stirs within it. In this it has company: the first flowering plants have also begun to move in. Bicolored lupines (*Lupinus micranthus*) begin to grow farther up the slope, closer to the burn. Because the seed's location was less scorched than areas higher up, the soil around it isn't as deficient in nitrogen as it might have been, and lupines thrive in nitrogen-deficient soil. Among them are the more common fireweed (*Epilobium angustifolium*), the same 3-meter (10-foot) plant that, much farther north, first recolonizes wet gravel left behind by retreating glaciers: it loves both fire and ice. Lupines and common fireweed grow abundantly throughout the valley after the burn, but down here on the gravel-bar the smaller, less-common broad-leaved fireweed (*E. latifolium*) is more at home. It grows to a height of only 30 centimeters (12 inches), but the color of its four-petaled pink flowers is deeper and more intense than that of its taller congener.

John Muir, walking through a clearing in the Douglas-fir forest of Oregon in 1888, wrote that he had stepped "into a charming wild garden full of lilies, orchids, heathworts, roses, etc., with colors so gay and forming such sumptuous masses of bloom, they make the gardens of civilization, however lovingly cared for, seem pathetic and silly," and it is reasonable to assume that some of those same wildflowers pioneered around our seed in 1300. The lilies might have been the Columbian lily (*Lilium columbianum*), better known as the tiger lily, which is found throughout the area, both in damp woods and in open meadows. Although its familiar orange petals with maroon spots don't appear until June, its stemless spears begin to pierce the soil in late April. The wood lily (*L. philadelphicum*) is also orange and maroon and also abundant in this area.

The orchids Muir saw are posers. Orchids are the largest of all plant groups, comprising more than thirty thousand species worldwide. Many are saprophytes, an extremely primitive group that feeds primarily on decaying vegetation and hence has no need of chlorophyll. No doubt one of Muir's orchids was the pink lady's slipper (*Calypso bulbosa*), also known as the deer-head orchid, which thrives on mossy forest floors in the perpetual shade of the giant trees. Lady's slippers entice bees into landing on the large, pouting lower lip of their pink flower, whereupon the upper lip closes, trapping the bee inside; as the bee struggles to extricate itself, it bangs into the flower's anther stem, picking up a cap of pollen, which, upon gaining its freedom, it may deposit on another flower.

Muir seems to have invented the term "heathworts," but the heath family includes such common plants as blueberry (*Vaccinium canadense*), wild buckwheat (*Eriogonum compositum*), and bearberry (*Arctostaphylos uva-ursi*), an evergreen shrub also known (by European traders and trappers, who brought the word west) as kinnikinnick, an Ojibway word for "mixture," because the leaves were dried and mixed with tobacco to make supplies last longer on extended journeys. The berries were also dried, pounded, mixed with salmon oil, and fried, so the name kinnikinnick might have made sense to the Coast Salish people who lived in the area. Muir describes the cassiope, another heather, as having "exceedingly slender creeping branches and scale-like leaves," a tiny plant that in July "spreads a wavering, interrupted belt of the loveliest bloom around glacier lakes and meadows and across wild moory expanses." And by roses Muir could have meant a whole host of plants, from true roses to the wild strawberry (*Fragaria virginiana*), the Indian plum, or osoberry (*Osmaronia cerasiformis*), and the imposing goatsbeard (*Aruncus sylvester*), all members of the Rosaceae family and all found in the cool, high woodlands of the Douglas-fir forest.

These flowering plants will not harm the Douglas-fir seed. Although when the tree reaches sapling height it will neither want nor tolerate much shade, as a seed it needs some protection from the burning sun. Like the seeds of all other types of trees, it already contains everything it needs to grow into a tree. It was fertilized before it left its cone. It has endured its necessary dormant winter stage. It is a vessel of hope, bearing all the accumulated genetic information necessary to carry out the metabolic processes of life. Rooted in one place, it must extract what else it needs to survive from that spot: carbon dioxide from the air, water and other elements from the soil, and light from the Sun.

It lies on the soil like a cocked pistol. Protected within its tough outer casing, or testa, and encased in its endosperm are an embryonic root, called the radicle; an embryonic stem, the hypocotyl; and five to seven embryonic leaves, or cotyledons. It has a larder of food stored in the endosperm and cotyledons, in the form of carbohydrates, to carry it through its first precarious days after being sparked into germination, which will nourish its growth until, as a seedling, it begins to photosynthesize.

As spring comes to the valley, two ravens take up residence in one of the intact Douglas-firs, higher up than the seed, and they often fly down to the stream to drink. Ravens (*Corvus corax*) are endlessly fascinating. They are the largest of the Corvidae, a group that includes crows, jays, and magpies, with wingspans of more than a meter (3 feet), making them bigger than many hawks. They will eat anything, including tree buds in winter, but they prefer meat. They rob other birds' nests of eggs and nestlings, especially in shorebird colonies. They will pick up an errant deer mouse or two. They spend a great deal of time strolling along the seashore or riverbank, picking at whatever living thing may be washed up. They attend all the fall salmon runs, shouldering bald eagles out of the way and rolling over stones with their beaks to get at fish eggs, which are packed with energy and nutrition. They build their untidy nests of sticks on cliff edges or high up in the tallest trees, which in the Douglas-fir forest is high up indeed, but they keep their baleful eyes to the ground, where their food is to be found. Their raucous, throaty calls are part of a surprisingly diverse operatic repertoire that includes clucks, plaintive wails, and a beautifully melodic gurgling song, the avian equivalent of Louis Armstrong suddenly launching into a song sounding like Bing Crosby.

Although definitely the loudest, theirs are not the only sounds in the valley; ravens are the brass section in an orchestra whose more delicate notes are provided by Swainson's thrushes, solitary vireos, yellow warblers, and other spring returnees. The yellow warblers are the Alaskan variety (*Dendroica petechia rubiginosa*), members of a highly vocal northern subspecies passing through on their way to the Aleutians and the Alaska Panhandle. They eat like nervous tourists, avoiding open spaces and the big trees to forage in the low broadleaf thickets along the streambed and around the edges of the regreening burn. They buzz the branches, hopping and hovering, plucking spider mites at a fantastic rate, their bright yellow tones shimmering in the sunlight.

A white-and-black pileated woodpecker (*Dryocopus pileatus*), looking startlingly like a flying fossil, perhaps an *Archeopteryx* with feathers magically restored, displays a consuming interest in carpenter ants but will not refrain from eating bark beetles, insects of the family that in the east are vectors of the deadly Dutch elm disease. Here they are represented by the ominously named Douglas-fir beetle (*Dendroctonus pseudotsugae*), a small, shiny black beetle that is especially attracted to healthy Douglas-firs that have been slightly damaged by fire. The females bore through the bark into the tree's cambium in the spring, eat out an ovipositional gallery that might be half a meter (1½ feet) long, and deposit their eggs in it; the eggs hatch after a few weeks and the larvae munch their way along new feeding galleries until they emerge in the fall as adults. The woodpecker, grasping the tree bark with its long talons and bracing itself with its tail, turns its head sideways as though listening for the sound of munching. In so doing it also keeps its eye open for flatheaded fir borers (*Melanophila drummondi*), the females of which don't dig into the tree but deposit their eggs in crevices in the bark, and the woodpecker easily spots their bronze-black, scarab-shaped bodies glinting in the sun.

THE ℬIRTH OF BOTANY

The ancient Greeks suspected that there was more to a tree than met the eye, and one of those whose recorded observations have been preserved was Theophrastus, whom Carolus Linneaus called the Father of Botany. Born on the island of Lesbos, now Myteline, in 371 BC, Theophrastus was sent to Athens as a youth to study under Plato. Upon Aristotle's death, Theophrastus inherited not only the Lyceum and its immense (and first) botanical garden, but also Aristotle's private library, reputed to have been the largest in Greece. Much of the information in Theophrastus's 227 botanical treatises and two books—*Historia Plantarum* and *De Causis Plantarum*—was almost certainly culled from Aristotle's own observations about the function, physiology, and meaning of plants.

Pileated woodpecker

Theophrastus improved and expanded upon these observations. He accepted little on faith and closely examined any information that came his way, be it from the lowliest of the *rhizotomi*—the root gatherers who supplied Athenian pharmacists with medicinal plants—or from the Master himself. Aristotle conjectured, for example, that trees lived on after being damaged because they contained some "vital principle" that existed in all parts of the tree, and that because of this universal life force they were forever "part dying and part being born." But to Aristotle, a tree was primarily a philosophical concept; he spoke not of particular trees but of the shadows of the Ideal Tree that flickered on the wall of Plato's cave. Aristotle wasn't what might be called a field scientist.

Theophrastus was. He went out and looked at plants. He dug them up and examined their roots. He dissected their seeds and fruits. He divided them into categories, as trees and shrubs and herbaceous plants, and remarked that while some trees grew in mountainous areas—he mentioned fir, wild pine, spruce, holly, box, walnut, and chestnut—others preferred the lowlands and plains: elm, ash, maple, willow, alder, and poplar. He believed that pines and firs thrived on sunny, south-facing slopes, whereas the hardwood trees grew better on the shadier sides of mountains. He saw that deciduous trees growing in cooler locales developed straight, unforked trunks, whereas those in full sun tended to divide into two or three trees joined at the base.

Although he accepted Aristotle's notion of a life force, as seen in a tree's ability to repair itself after injury or even survive out of the ground, Theophrastus also examined how that force was transmitted into the many parts of the tree. He recognized the root as "that part of the tree by which aliment is taken" and the stem as the vessel through which that nourishment is delivered to the leaves. He could think of no useful purpose for leaves and wondered whether they were true organs or mere appendages, but he described hundreds of them, using their patterns as a way of distinguishing between different species or of lumping seemingly dissimilar plants into a common genus. He divided species into binomial categories—that is, using double-barrelled names. He wrote about seed germination and the development of seedlings, correctly determining that the radicle stirred within the seed coat first and then the stem. Theophrastus was a genuine observational field scientist, and his authority in matters botanical extended into the Middle Ages and beyond; at the time our tree was beginning its life, what Theophrastus knew about plant morphology was still as much as anyone knew, and probably more.

The second great name in Greek botany is Dioscorides. Born in Cilicia, along the Mediterranean coast, around the time of Christ, he was a physician in the Roman army and in AD 50 was probably in Egypt, where he would have had access to the now-lost library of Alexandria. His only written work, *De materia medica*, discusses the pharmaceutical properties of more than six hundred plants and seems to have been written as a guide for doctors and even ordinary citizens, unlike the more scholarly work of Theophrastus. Dioscorides was not so much interested in why plants had healing powers as he was in informing people of their preparation and most effective application.

Many of Dioscorides' herbal remedies are still in use, among them almond oil, aloe, belladonna, calamine, ginger, juniper, marjoram, and opium. He also described drugs derived from animals and minerals. The work of Dioscorides was cited as the ultimate authority on herbal medicines well into the seventeenth century, even by physicians living in northern Europe, where few of the plants he described were found. *De materia medica* became as much a part of medical doctrine as the Bible was of religious dogma. The book, in various Latin translations, was constantly available as a major reference; in 1300, the Italian natural historian Pietro d'Abano lectured on Dioscorides in Paris and, later, upon returning to Padua, fervently espoused Dioscorides' insistence on looking for the natural causes of all natural phenomena—so fervently, in fact, that he was charged with heresy for questioning the miraculousness of Christ's birth, although he died before the case came to trial. His fate illustrates not only the growing rift between science and religion but also the far-reaching effects the simple study of plants can have in seemingly unrelated areas. Forty years after his death in 1315, d'Abano's writings were condemned and his body was disinterred and burned.

BENEATH THE SHELTER of the wildflowers' first leaves, the seed begins the alchemical process of absorbing the basic elements of air, sunlight, and water and turning them into life. All it needs to get started is a little warmth and moisture, which on a south-facing slope in the Puget Trough in the Pacific Northwest is not a bad definition of spring.

T A K I N G R O O T

I am the voice of wind
And wave and tree,
Of stern desires and blind,
Of strength to be . . .
CHARLES G.D. ROBERTS, "Autochton"

*H*igh on the south-facing slope where our seed has lodged, water, warmth, and oxygen are present in abundance. The seed is surrounded by stirring life. Like particles of dust lit by shafts of sunlight, insects emerge from the forest floor and flash briefly through the slivers of light filtered through the canopy. The thrum of their calls fills the air. Like some mythical serpent, bracken ferns (*Pteridium aquilinum*) begin to unwind their coiled heads and stretch their enormous fronds. Pockets of ocean spray

(*Holodiscus discolor*) are sprouting; they will achieve heights of 3 to 4 meters (10 to 13 feet), and their long branches already droop with luscious, cream-colored blossoms. Life in the Douglas-fir forest is not only abundant but large.

Our seed is now fully awake, its juices flowing and its engine purring. The radicle stirs within the testa. It is the first part of the plant to emerge, threading its way through a small opening, or micropyle, in the seed coat. It wears a root cap, a loosely fitting cellular hard hat that protects the root's delicate tip from being damaged as it insinuates itself downward through the rough soil. The root grows by adding more of itself through cell division behind the cap; cells within the root also differentiate into distinct types of tissue. The center, or core, contains the xylem, which is tissue made up of stacks of connected, hollow, elongated cells called tracheids. Each tracheid, closed at either end like a tiny capsule, exists for support and to carry water, which enters the xylem through the root wall, or endodermis. The water seeps through pits in the walls of the tracheids and then passes into the next tracheid up the chain and so to the rest of the plant.

The mechanism for water transfer in a tree is not fully understood. In a grown tree, tracheid columns extend from the roots to the canopy, lifting water more than 100 meters (330 feet) from the ground. In thin straws, water may be pulled up the sides by surface tension, in what is called capillary action, but this process can lift water only a few millimeters. Osmosis, the tendency of water to move from a dilute condition toward a solution more concentrated in salts, explains the pull of water from the soil into the root cells, but how it is drawn up from there to the leaves or needles is still a mystery. The currently favored hypothesis is that evaporation from the leaves creates a vacuum behind it, and the vacuum draws water up through the xylem. There may also be pumping mechanisms whereby water molecules are actively pushed or pulled. When a xylem column is punctured—by tunneling insects, for example—air intrudes and the column ceases to lift water for the rest of the tree's life.

The second type of tissue is the phloem. Phloem is like xylem but is made up of sieve cells that are also linked end-to-end along the root stem; sieve cells perform a similar function to that of tracheids in the xylem, except that the liquid flows in both directions, transferring nutrients stored in the cotyledons (and later manufactured in the leaves or needles) down to the roots. Tracheids and sieve cells are the up-and-down elevators in a skyscraping tree.

A SECRET LIFE

Our tree has begun its secret life. Secret to us, at any rate, since after millennia of study there is still much about a tree we do not know. There are physical questions—how many different types of hormones it produces, for example. But there are also less tangible areas of inquiry. Is a tree a solitary entity, or does it achieve its true nature through association with other individual plants and animals? Scientists suspect there is truth in both possibilities.

Trees are communal, sometimes to the point of being communistic: they grow together in large groups, as though for comfort or protection. They have relationships—including sexual relationships through cross-pollination—and even communicate with other trees within their stands, including trees of their own kind as well as those of other species; they function for the benefit of the whole in sometimes startling ways; and they enter into mutualistic partnerships with other species—even other species so distantly related they belong to different orders—as surely as human beings raise beans for food. "Far more than ourselves," writes John Fowles in *The Tree*, "trees are social creatures and no more natural as isolated specimens than man is as a marooned sailor or hermit." To understand a single tree, we must understand the entire forest.

But some trees *are* marooned sailors. When Mark Twain paddled his canoe to a volcanic island in the middle of Mono Lake in California, just east of what is now Yosemite National Park, in 1865, he found a landscape entirely devastated by repeated volcanic eruptions, "nothing but gray ashes and pumice stone," he wrote, "in which we sunk to our knees at every step." He had never seen a more desolate, lifeless terrain. The center of the island was "a shallow, far-reaching basin, carpeted with ashes, and here and there a patch of fine sand." Close to a jet of steam still emanating from the active volcano, however, he discovered "the only tree on the island, a small pine of most graceful shape and most faultless symmetry." The tree was actually benefiting from being close to the volcano, "for the steam drifted unceasingly through its branches and kept them always moist." There can be no more compelling testament to the persistence of life, and of life individually sustained, than that solitary pine in that infernally blasted basin.

Sociable though it is, then, a tree is also intensely individualistic, in that, ultimately, any life-or-death directions a tree takes throughout its lifetime will unthinkingly be taken in favor of its own survival and that of its offspring. In matters of survival, a tree is a closed system. Given its initial luck in landing in a situation favorable to growth, each tree has or can obtain for itself everything it needs to further its own simple but specific ends, which are to live long enough and be healthy enough to produce offspring that will launch some of its hereditary material into the future. A forest is not merely a crowd of trees, it is a community of many organisms. But each individual in it can distinguish what Fowles calls "the single from the ruck." From a Douglas-fir's point of view, the ruck is what fires take care of.

A TREE IS PART of a community, but a tree itself is also a community of disparate parts—roots, stem, branches, needles, cones, inner core, outer bark. Its self-sufficiency comes from having worked out over time a network connecting all of its members more or less constantly. Not only does it need to get water from the ground to the leaves and nutrients from the leaves to the roots, but other compounds may have to be moved efficiently as well, perhaps even more efficiently than water and food.

For example, it can take a mature Douglas-fir thirty-six hours to lift water from its roots to its canopy; compounds to repel an insect invasion or heal a broken limb may have to get there more quickly. The human body has a number of systems for different parts to communicate and transfer information: a central nervous system, a sympathetic nervous system, a lymphatic system, an immune system. Trees have been around a lot longer than humans, indeed a lot longer than mammals—there are far more plant species on Earth than species of mammal; in fact, there are almost as many *orchid* species alone as there are mammalian species—and have also evolved their own complex systems for regulating growth, maintenance, repair, and defense. Theophrastus was not far wrong when he speculated that a tree had a "vital principle" flowing through its veins; nor was British botanist Nehemiah Grew, who wrote in *The Anatomy of Plants* in 1682 that pollen "falls down upon the seed case or womb and touches it with a prolific virtue and vivific effluvia." Both writers were trying to express their sense of the mysterious inner life force that generates a tree but it is only recently that we have actually gained a window into this force.

The first "vivific effluvia" to be scientifically verified in a tree's secret system were auxins, plant growth hormones that stimulate cells to divide, enlarge, and differentiate. Julius von Sachs, the great German plant physiologist and theorist, was the first to demonstrate that plant seeds store nutrients in the form of starch, that starch is the first detectable product of photosynthesis, and that cell enlargement was more important than cell division in root formation. In 1865 he suggested that "specific organ-forming substances" responsible for the formation of flowers and seeds were produced in the leaves. Although he never succeeded in isolating or even identifying these substances, his influence was so great that he set an entire generation of botanical scientists looking for them and ultimately verifying his predictions.

Eureka came in the 1920s from a group of researchers working at the University of Utrecht, in Holland, under Dutch botanist Friedrich Went. The Utrecht School set out to understand the concept of tropism in plants—what it was that made plants respond to various external influences, such as light (phototropism), water (aquatropism), and gravity (geotropism). How, they wondered, does a plant's root always grow downward when it emerges from a seed, even if the seed has landed upside down? Traditional theory had it that the root was geotropic—its own weight pulled it down. But if that were the case, they reasoned, then what caused the root to stop growing down and start growing horizontally? Although most trees, including Douglas-fir, have a central, carrotlike taproot, more than 90 percent of a tree's root system is spread laterally within a quarter of a meter (9 inches) of the surface. And if plants were geotropic, what impelled a plant's stem to always grow upward, against gravity?

The Utrecht School discovered that plant organs, notably the leaves and buds, produce hormones—auxins—that travel down the plant's stem along with nutrients in the phloem and concentrate in areas requiring rapid cell growth. In young trees like ours, those places are behind the root cap and in the embryonic stem, or plumule, which in the seedling is now beginning to show signs of life.

Auxins travel from the seed case down the root core as well as into the young embryonic stem, but they do not distribute evenly throughout the cells of either structure; rather, being large molecules and therefore subject to gravity, they concentrate in the lower halves, like sand mixed in water traveling in a horizontal pipe. Then three special properties of auxins come into play. First, the right concentration of auxins promotes cell division and therefore growth, but too high a concentration inhibits growth. Second, it takes a much smaller concentration of auxins to affect the growth of the root than of the stem. And third, sunlight lowers the ability of auxins to promote cell division. All three properties combined explain how a root always grows downward, while a stem always grows upward. Auxins in the root concentrate in the bottom half in such high concentrations that they inhibit division of the auxin-sensitive cells; therefore, the top half of the root, with lower amounts of auxins, grows faster than the bottom half, and the root curves downward. Meanwhile, auxins accumulated in the bottom part of the tree's plumule promote growth, while sunlight falling on the top half of the plumule inhibits growth, and so the plumule shoots upward. As a result, there is a seedling with its root growing downward and its stem rising up toward the sun. As it stretches, its auxins become more evenly distributed, so the stem straightens.

Plant hormones occur in many different forms. One is indoleacetic acid, which fruit growers spray on trees to promote uniform growth. Ethylene is another type of hormone, which is also used to hasten the ripening of fruit. The synthetic herbicide 2,4-D is yet another auxin; it kills some broadleaf plants and spares others. A related auxin, 2,4,5-T, contains dioxin, a compound that causes miscarriage, birth defects, and organ dysfunction in humans: 2,4-D mixed with 2,4,5-T is called Agent Orange.

FOR CENTURIES, natural philosophers puzzled over the difference between living beings and inanimate objects. What distinguishes life from nonlife? As we have seen, life began as a coagulation of nonliving molecules. Vitalists believed that there was some inspiriting force present in living organisms, some physical substance that animated nonliving matter and exited upon death. They weighed a living organism, killed it, and weighed it again, attempting to ascertain whether the vital force had mass that could be detected. In fact, air was often referred to as spirit, as without air there was no life. Echoes of that sense are still present in English: to inspire is to take in air, but it is also to give a creative boost; to expire is both to exhale and to die.

Early chemists understood that life was based on molecules of proteins, nucleic acids, lipids, and carbohydrates—all built around carbon. They assumed that only living organisms could create these complex, carbon-based molecules, an assumption that persisted until 1828, when German chemist Fritz Haber took ammonium and cyanate and synthesized urea, an organic compound found in urine. A few years later, his student Hermann Kolbe made acetic acid, another organic compound. Clearly, test-tube chemistry could duplicate the chemical processes of life.

When Sir Isaac Newton (1642–1727) revolutionized physics with his studies of optics and gravity, he perceived the universe as an immense mechanical construct, a giant clockwork that scientists could probe by analyzing its various parts. He inaugurated a new scientific methodology, known as reductionism. According to the assumptions underlying this approach, insights gained by studying bits and pieces of nature could be fitted together like pieces of a jigsaw puzzle to eventually explain the workings of the cosmos. Reductionism has been a powerful tool for obtaining and examining information from nature. But as scientists investigated the parts of living organisms, they found the parts themselves were made up of parts—molecules—which were in turn assemblages of atoms, which were ultimately made up of quarks, the (so far) irreducible structures of all matter. At the quark level, there was nothing to distinguish life from nonlife. Nothing in these most elementary structures could provide insights into the appearance of complex processes of development, differentiation, or consciousness. Modern biology and medicine continue to operate on the reductionist assumption, examining the pieces in the belief that they can be added together to explain the whole.

Life itself is a refutation of reductionism, testimony that wholes are greater than the sum of their parts. For one thing, the appearance of life from nonlife indicates that if there is no vital force or spirit present in the ultimate particles of matter, then life must result from the collective interaction of nonliving parts, a synergy that produces such emergent properties as respiration, digestion, and reproduction.

FABULOUS *Fungi*

"We have now arrived," Alexandre Dumas writes in his *Grand dictionnaire de cuisine* in 1869, "at the *sacrum sacrorum* of the gastronomes, at the name never pronounced by a gourmand without touching his hat—the *Tuber cibarium*, the *Lycoperdon gulosorum*, the truffle."

To write the history of the truffle, Dumas continues, would be to undertake the history of civilization, which he then proceeds to do. Truffles were known to the Romans, he says, but before that were eaten by the Greeks, who got them from Libya. It seems they were never out of fashion. When the English diarist John Evelyn, author of *Sylva, or a Discourse of Forest Trees,* traveled in France in 1644, he noted in his diary a stop in the province of Dauphine, where he "supp'd, having (amongst other dainties) a dish of Truffles, which is a certaine earth-nut, found out by an hogg, train'd up to it, and for which those Creatures are sold at a greate price."

Dumas' *Tuber cibarium* is actually the true gourmand's truffle, *T. aestivum*, but his *Lycoperdon gulosorum* is more likely *L. gemmatum*, the gemmed puffball, which is knobby like a truffle and edible when young. After the sows rooted up truffles (only female pigs could be trained to do this), the mushrooms were either blended with goose liver to make pâté de foie gras or else cooked in a number of intriguing ways. The truffle was more than a fad; in Europe, it became the symbol of French cultural superiority. And as a supposed aphrodisiac, truffles were right up there with oysters and absolute power. "Sensual men of fashion," wrote a fifteenth-century Italian socialite, "consume them to whet their appetite for love-making." As it turns out, truffles really are an aphrodisiac, at least for sows: they are now known to contain twice as much of the male hormone androsterone as the average boar, and so female pigs who snout them up probably think they are in for more than a good meal.

Having a fruit that smells strongly of male hormones is part of the fungus's reproductive strategy. A truffle is stuffed with spores, and when the spores are ready to be released to the air, a difficult feat for an underground organism, the truffle releases its andro-steroid pheromone and some female animal—in the woods, bears, porcupines, and mice do not need to be trained—comes along, digs it up, eats it, and defecates the spores, which, protected by a tough outer coat, have passed undigested through the animal's gut: emission accomplished.

Toward the end of the nineteenth century, the King of Prussia asked mycologist A.B. Hatch to figure out a way to grow truffles domestically and thus wrest the truffle trade away from France, which relied on wild truffles. Like a paleontologist uncovering a cache of crisscrossing bones, Hatch carefully exhumed an underground fungal system. He discovered that the parent fungi were not growing through the soil alone; they attached themselves to the fine roots of the trees that grew around them—in this case, primarily oaks. Fungus and root actually grew into one another until they seemed to become almost a single organism. Hatch named this compound life-form mycorrhizae, which means fungus-root. He pondered the nature of such a peculiar association; except for truffles and other edible fungi, humans have an antagonistic relationship with fungus. We associate it with rot and disease—and rightly so. Apart from such relatively minor fungal-generated problems as athlete's foot, yeast infections, and dandruff, various fungi are also responsible for three kinds of pneumonia and one kind of meningitis. And many plant diseases are caused by fungal invasions. Our impulse is to think that a plant root "infected" by a fungus would sicken and die. But in a mycorrhizal arrangement, both fungus and root benefit from the experience.

Hatch's work was followed up in the 1880s by that of French scientist Louis Alexandre Mangin, who was interested in plant respiration and root development. Mangin observed that certain fungi seemed to have a special affinity with specific plants; some were found only on tree roots, whereas others seemed to prefer herbaceous plants. A few years later, while investigating the propagation of orchids, another French botanist, Bernard Noël, took the mycorrhizal relationship a giant step forward when he determined that all orchids depended on fungi for their supply of nutrients—in other words, among the oldest lineage of plants on Earth, the mycorrhizal relationship was obligatory, for without their fungal partners, orchids wither and die.

It is now believed that almost all mycorrhizal relationships are, if not a requirement, then certainly the norm; very few plant species grow without a fungal partner, and those that have them grow better for it. Fossil evidence suggests that this mutual dependency existed 400 million years ago, in the first plants to invade the continents. "In fact," writes Chris Maser, "land plants probably originated through a symbiosis between marine fungi and photosynthesizing algae." Since the marine plants that invaded the land had no roots of their own, they would have had to make use of fungi to obtain enough water and minerals to survive on dry land. The fungi, for their part, needed the plants for the food they produced by photosynthesis.

Fungi, of which there are some ninety thousand species, are incapable of manufacturing their own food internally, since they have no chloroplasts, as other plants do. However, they still require energy in the form of sugars in order to reproduce, and so mycorrhizal fungi penetrate the roots of living plants and take sugar from the plant host. In fact, they take so much sugar that they are able to expand to gigantic proportions. If that were the end of the story, the fungus would be a parasite and the tree would eventually die. But the fungus reciprocates the favor; in return for the sugars it derives from the tree, its vast network of hyphae provides the tree's root system with access to water and nutrients it would not otherwise be able to reach or extract from the mineral matrix.

A tree is stuck where its seed landed and sent down its original root, fixing its fate to a single spot. After that the tree cannot dodge predators or pests, seek food elsewhere, or migrate to a more benign climate. Its expanding root system will have to find water and dissolved nutrients, as well as anchor the growing plant against wind, rain, and floods. The efficiency of the roots depends on the distance they penetrate into the soil as well as on the surface area that comes into contact with the material in the ground. The mat of fungal hyphae vastly increases the volume of soil a tree is able to explore. It absorbs water and passes it on to the tree. Hyphae are also better than tree roots at extracting critical nutrients from soil, such as phosphorus and nitrogen, which they then trade to the tree in exchange for sugar. They excrete enzymes that break down nitrogen in the soil and sometimes even kill insects and absorb trace elements from their bodies, which are then passed along to the tree.

Fungi/orchid relationships are endotrophic, which means the fungus actually penetrates and grows inside cells of the orchid's tuber. Nearly 300,000 plant species have endotrophic mycorrhizal relationships with only 130 species of fungi. Fungi/tree relationships are ectotrophic, since the complex network of hyphae, called the mycelium, forms a mantle that encases the root on the outside, like a layer of gauze, and also fills the spaces between the cells of the root's cortex without penetrating them, forming what is called a Hartig net. As Jon Luoma notes in *The Hidden Forest*, "mycologists now believe that mycorrhizal fungi effectively connect trees with as much as one thousand times more soil area than the roots themselves." And within that area the concentration of hyphae is immense. A single liter of soil from a mycorrhizal mass contains several kilometers of tightly compacted hyphae. Only about 2,000 plant species are ectomycorrhizal, but they involve some 5,000 species of fungi.

Mycorrhizal fungi confer tremendous resilience on their host trees in the face of droughts, floods, high temperatures, a paucity of soil nutrients, low oxygen, and other possible sources of stress. Studies show that fungi even protect trees from invasion by other, potentially harmful fungi: when red pine is inoculated with the mycorrhizal fungus *Paxillus involutus*, for example, the *Paxillus*

Mycorrhizal fungi

produces an antimicrobial fungitoxin that makes the tree almost twice as resistant to *Fusarium* root rot as it would otherwise be. It pays a fungus to keep its sugar source happy and healthy so that it will continue to pump out sugar.

Douglas-firs enter into ectomycorrhizal relationships with more than two thousand species of fungi. A single tree may have several kinds of fungi attached to different parts of its root system, especially if the roots extend into different soil types. Some fungi are associated with certain tree species. *Suillus lakei*, or the painted Suillus, for example, is a reddish-brown mushroom found almost exclusively under Douglas-firs; it is edible, although it can get somewhat viscid late in the season. The purple *Laccaria* is also partial to Douglas-fir shade, although it is also found under pines and other woody plants.

Perhaps the most unusual partnership between a plant and a fungus is that between the Indian pipe (*Monotropa uniflora*), a flowering plant, and the *Boletus* fungus that attaches to its roots. Indian pipe grows in moist woodlands across North America, including the Pacific Northwest—there are specimens all around our tree, their faintly pink stems and bowed heads poking up like pale, sad worms above the forest litter. Since it has no chlorophyll of its own (it turns black as it matures), it does not produce sugars either for itself or for its mycorrhizal partner, and yet *Boletus* is there. It turns out that the fungus attached to the Indian pipe roots also attaches to the roots of nearby conifers, such as Douglas-fir; the *Boletus* siphons nutrients out of the conifer and transfers them directly to the Indian pipe. No one knows what, if anything, the Indian pipe contributes to the fungus or to the Douglas-fir. It might contribute nothing; if so, this is one of the rare instances in nature of a free lunch.

FROM FERTILE 🖉OIL

Ideas, like trees, need nutrient-rich ground in which to prosper and even then may take almost as much time as a Douglas-fir to come to fruition. Throughout the first half of the thirteenth century, a revolution in scientific thinking took place in Europe under the enlightened patronage of the Holy Roman Emperor Frederick II. During the Dark Ages, the works of the ancient Greeks had been lost or banned by the Church, and Roman thinkers had contributed little of significance to the advancement of scientific learning. Under Frederick II's reign, Greek texts were rediscovered, translated into Latin, and made available to an increasingly literate population. They included works by Aristotle, Euclid, Ptolemy, Archimedes, Diocles, and Galen. Arabian works on medicine, astronomy, optics, and chemistry were also read and discussed, largely through Latin translations. For more than twelve hundred years of Roman ecclesiastical suppression, the "scientific" texts approved by the Church had been mainly cobbled-together encyclopedias and herbals like that of Dioscorides—lists of medicinal plants, many of which had never been seen north of the Mediterranean. During the thirteenth century, the natural sciences suddenly exploded into the popular imagination.

The most widely respected scholar to flourish under Frederick II was Albertus Magnus, or Albert the Great, who was revered as a magician in his days at court, when alchemy and astrology were considered legitimate scientific pursuits. His book *De Vegetabilus et Plantis,* published in 1250—the year of Frederick II's death— was a commentary on *De Vegetabilus,* a compilation by Theophrastus of works believed to have been written by Aristotle. Albertus's version included vivid descriptions of native plants not known to the Greeks, as well as his own observations when he disagreed with those of the original author. He valued curiosity and experience (the word in Latin is *experimenta*)—the two pillars of scientific enquiry. On dissecting a tree, he declared that sap was carried by special veins from the roots to the leaves—like blood vessels, he said, but without the pulse.

At the time of Albertus's death in 1280, Frederick II had been dead for thirty years and Edward I was king of England. The most accomplished English scientist of Edward's reign was Roger Bacon, who was born in 1219 and received his master's degree from Oxford University in 1240. After graduation he lectured for a time in Paris, as a member of the Franciscan order, on the works of Aristotle.

Like Albertus, Bacon extolled the virtues of what he called "experimental science," the physical study of natural phenomena, rather than a reliance on abstract reasoning or received wisdom. And like Pietro d'Abano, he repudiated authority and therefore came into conflict with the Church—late in his life he was imprisoned in Paris by his own Franciscan order for his "suspect novelties" and "dangerous doctrines," possibly stemming from his admiration for the great Arabian philosopher Averroës, who preached a doctrine of Universal Reason on Aristotelian grounds but denied the immortality of individual souls. But Bacon took Europe another step along the path out of the Dark Ages and away from the unquestioning adherence to dogma, whether religious or scientific. "For authors write many statements," he maintained, "and people believe them through reasoning which they formulate without experience. Their reasoning is wholly false."

Just as our tree is taking its first tentative probes into the soil, the world of science is also at the dawn of a new way of investigating the secrets of nature.

UP FROM 𝒰NDERGROUND

The tree's young root establishes its own ectomycorrhizal relationships beneath the warm summer soil, and its stem begins to
waver upward. It does not emerge from the seed coat so much as
rise up with the seed coat perched on its head like a World War I
pilot's helmet. With only the beginning of nodes on which it will
eventually grow needles, it is still dependent on starch stored in
the endosperm and cotyledons for energy. When this stored energy is exhausted, the endosperm will soon drop away, and then
the stem will have to produce needles to keep its roots and fungal
partners supplied with food.

The stem's internal structure is very much like that of the
root—xylem and phloem, encased in an epidermis—except that
the stem's outer layer is not porous, as the root's must be. It is bark,
albeit a thin, grayish, wispy kind of bark this early in life. A grown
tree is essentially dead heartwood surrounded by ten to fifteen
years' worth of living sapwood, casketed in a layer of living tissue
called the cambium. As new tracheids form under the inner bark,
the old cells die and the tree becomes bigger in diameter. Think of
a candle getting thicker by being dipped again and again in hot
wax. In a tree, the new layer of hot wax is the cambium, and the
layers of cooled wax are the tree's heartwood, the rings of its earlier growth. If a nail were driven into the trunk of our tree when it
is 10 meters (33 feet) tall, the nail would still be the same distance
from the ground when the tree is fully grown; a tree increases its
height at the top, while the trunk gains only in girth. At the moment, the tree is all living matter, all cambium, sapwood, and bark,
with no central dead core. Water from the roots moves up the stem
through the xylem's tracheids, and when the first needles form and
start photosynthesizing, starch—which is condensed sugar—will

move down the stem through the phloem's sieve cells to be stored and used in the roots.

As in all trees, the young Douglas-fir's xylem cells are composed of nuclei surrounded by thick walls of cellulose, and they run up the core of the stem like a bundle of segmented plastic straws. Cellulose is a polysaccharide, composed of repeating units of the simple sugars glucose and fructose. It is soft when formed in the protoplast but hardens when it reaches the cell wall. It is the most abundant organic polymer known. All plants have it; even some fungi have it in the walls of their hyphae. It is also one of the toughest of natural fibers, more stress resistant—and, as herbivores know, more indigestible—than silk, tendon, or even bone. Its strength is due in part to hydrogen bonding within each molecule as well as between parallel molecules. Cellulose is so strongly bonded, in fact, that without auxins to break down the bonds, not even new cellulose molecules would attach to them on the inside surface of the wall, and the tree would not grow.

An additional cell component is lignin, the second-most-abundant plant polymer, which adds firmness and strength to the cell walls. When plants first invaded the land and some of them began to rise above their fellow plants, their stems were composed of cells with walls made up of only cellulose. As they grew higher, many of them would snap off in the wind or collapse under their own weight; those that did not had, by some unknown process, acquired lignin, which acts in the cell walls like rebar in concrete. Eventually only plants with lignin survived to produce offspring. Wood is now about 65 percent cellulose and 35 percent lignin.

Lignin is a linkage of three aromatic alcohols—coumaryl, coniferyl, and sinapyl—which fill the spaces in cell walls that are not already occupied by other substances, even ousting water molecules to do so. It thus forms a very strong hydrophobic net, cementing all the cell-wall elements in place and providing strength and rigidity to the xylem. It also provides an important barrier to fungal and bacterial infections. When a tree is invaded by disease, it seals off the infected section with a wall of lignin so that the disease cannot spread. Lignin is so tough that getting rid of it is a costly process in pulp-and-paper plants. The acids needed to break down lignin in pulpwood are the chief pollutants such mills contribute to the environment.

Near the tip of our young tree, five cotyledons have spread out from the stem like the ribs of a green umbrella. They are the tree's first needles. At the top, where they join the stem, is a rounded protuberance called the apical meristem, and it is here that new growth occurs. The meristem features a series of tiny bumps, or nodes, and at each node a new spray of needles will form. At first the nodes are close together, but gradually the cells within the meristem divide and expand, and the distance between the nodes increases. Above some of the nodes, lateral or axillary buds appear. These will eventually produce branches, and each branch tip will have its own apical meristem. In hardwoods such as oak or maple, axillary buds appear above each leaf node, but in Douglas-fir and other softwoods the nodes are so close together—the internodal distance is only 2 millimeters (less than $\frac{1}{10}$ inch)—that buds appear only at a small proportion of nodes. Each bud is a tiny, compressed shoot composed of embryonic leaves, nodes, and internodes, lying dormant and ready for a boost of food from the roots to begin developing into branches.

With its cotyledons fanned out at the tip and supported by an irregular stem, the Douglas-fir now looks like a tiny palm tree. Although diminutive, it is a fully functioning organism; at each of its meristems its cells are dividing and expanding like mad, and its seed leaves are already performing the lifelong process of photosynthesis.

There are now many cells throughout the tree, each performing its own individual, preassigned task. For a plant, as for animals, multicellularity has conferred the opportunity to develop a diversity of functions within a single organism. As we have seen, a multicellular organism is essentially a colony of smaller organisms. This diversity, however, presents a biological paradox. How did it arise? Mitosis, or the process of cell division, ensures that the genetic makeup of all daughter cells will be identical. If development and differentiation of cell and tissue types are under genetic control, what is the mechanism that produces the differences?

Molecular biology, through a series of elegant experiments, has shown that fertilization combines parental chromosomes to form the genome, which is then replicated faithfully with every cell division. The genome of a fertilized egg may be seen as a blueprint designating the processes that eventually lead to an individual whose many cells function smoothly in their roles. A DNA blueprint, however, is too immense for any one cell to read in its entirety. Instead, as cell division proceeds, each daughter cell receives molecular signals that direct it to read only specific sections of the blueprint—the section on root production, for example. But what are the signals that tell a particular cell what to read, and can we manipulate them? The recent discovery in mammals of stem cells that are "totipotent," that have the ability to differentiate into any cell type, may lead to such applications as the regeneration of lost limbs or even entire organs, when those cellular signals are better understood.

A LEAF WITH THE *L*IGHT ON IT

Photosynthesis is the process that makes the diversity and abundance of life on Earth possible. Although it was no secret that plants derived their energy from the Sun and their nourishment from the soil—Leonardo da Vinci, in his *Notebooks,* correctly wrote that "the sun gives spirit and life to plants, and the earth nourishes them with moisture"—understanding how the process works is a relatively recent development. In 1779, Jan Ingen-Housz, a Dutch plant physiologist, published his monumentally titled *Experiments Upon Vegetables, Discovering their Great Power of Purifying the Common Air in the Sunshine and of Injuring It in the Shade and at Night.* He had been following up on experiments conducted by the great English chemist and theologian Joseph Priestley, the author of numerous articles on religion and the discoverer of oxygen. Priestley had begun his studies of "inflammable air" in 1766. By 1775 he had determined that plants could restore an atmosphere that had been made unfit to breathe by combustion or putrefaction by supplying it with "dephlogisticated air," later defined as oxygen.

This early appreciation of the importance of plants to human life so intrigued Ingen-Housz that he moved from Holland to England to be closer to Priestley and his coterie of experimental chemists. In his own experiments, he discovered that only the green parts of plants purified air by producing oxygen and that, moreover, these green parts also removed carbon not from soil, as had been previously maintained, but from air. He realized that animals and plants mutually benefited one another, the one by breathing in oxygen and expelling carbon dioxide, the other by removing carbon dioxide from the air and replenishing it with oxygen. As a doctor—in Holland he had developed a vaccine against smallpox and in 1768 had personally inoculated the royal house of Austria—and with his new knowledge of plant function, he helped patients who had respiratory illnesses by placing them, during daylight hours, in rooms filled with green plants, and at night—when photosynthesis stopped—by replacing the plants with an apparatus of his own design that produced pure oxygen.

A conifer needle is just such an apparatus. An evergreen needle and a deciduous leaf, though constructed differently, contain many of the same components and perform in similar ways; their shapes differ because their environments create different requirements for efficiency. It is difficult to generalize about the advantages of decid-uous versus evergreen. Both types of trees are found in a wide variety of environments. But for the most part, deciduous trees are adapted to climates with long, cold winters or to seasonally dry climates at lower latitudes; dropping their leaves in the fall and growing new ones each spring costs less energy than maintaining leaves through extended subzero temperatures. A needle, with its small surface area, transpires less water than a broadleaf and so works well in environments with a lot of sun and long dry periods, as is the case around the Mediterranean Sea and on the western slopes of North America.

Too much sunlight inhibits photosynthesis, and Douglas-fir is a canopy species, which means its upper branches receive a lot of sun. Its conical shape also ensures that each new level of branches does not cast the lower branches into shade. Needles are also bet-ter at shedding snow than broadleaves, and so there is less danger of broken branches. And needles contain little sap, meaning that they are more resistant to freezing. A mature Douglas-fir may have 65 million needles, and they all work all the time, but no single needle gets too much light.

Unlike leaves, which drop off after one season, needles on most conifers stay on for two or three years—some evergreens, such as the monkey puzzle tree, keep their leaves for up to fifteen years; the needles on bristlecone pines stay on for fifty years—so trees have longer to store up the energy needed to replace them. And they produce more energy. By keeping their needles year round, conifers can photosynthesize nonstop even during the winter months, when light levels as well as temperatures drop dramatically. A study conducted in Germany comparing the energy produced and stored by a deciduous tree (in this case, beech) with that of a conifer (Norway spruce) found that the beech photosynthesized for 176 days in one year, whereas the Norway spruce photosynthesized for 260; even with its smaller total leaf surface area, the spruce was 58 percent more productive than the beech.

A Douglas-fir needle is flat, rectangular in cross section, and composed of an epidermis within which are found the photosynthesizing cells. Deciduous leaves and some conifer needles, including those of Douglas-fir, contain two types of cells: palisade mesophyll cells, which are attached to the inside of the epidermis, and loosely packed spongy mesophyll cells. In Douglas-fir, the pallisade cells on the upper surface of the needles protect the spongy cells from too much light. Holes in the needle's epidermis, called stomata, are opened and closed by two guard cells. *Stoma* is the Greek word for throat (and so is misused in the English word *stomach*). A broad leaf, such as that of an elm or a maple, has millions of stomata, usually on the underside of the leaf; the leaves of some oaks have 100,000 stomata per square centimeter of leaf surface. A Douglas-fir needle has fewer stomata, but they are also located on the underside. The guard cells act like lips; they swell and contract according to how much water there is in the needle, thereby controlling the amount of carbon dioxide entering through the stomata and the amount of oxygen and water vapor that diffuse out from the needle.

A tree can lift and transpire vast amounts of water. A single tree in the Amazon rain forest lifts hundreds of liters of water every day. The rain forest behaves like a green ocean, transpiring water that rains upward, as though gravity were reversed. These transpired mists then flow across the continent in great rivers of vapor. The water condenses, falls as rain, and is pulled back up again through the trees. It rises and falls on its westward migration an average of six times before finally hitting the physical barrier of the Andes mountains and flowing back across the continent as the mightiest river on Earth. Similarly, Indonesia, with 114 million hectares (28 million acres) of tropical forest (it is the second most forested country in the world after Brazil) is a vital part of the Asian hydrologic cycle. Around the world, forests constantly replenish Earth's supply of fresh water and play a key role in weather and climate.

Plants are also a rich source of molecules that people have learned to exploit over thousands of years. In 1817, two French chemists—Pierre-Joseph Pelletier, who was an assistant professor of the natural history of drugs at Paris's École de Pharmacie, and Joseph Bienaimé Caventou, a graduate student—were studying alkaloids and plant coloring agents. As well as discovering the alkaloids strychnine, quinine, and caffeine, they determined that the green pigment in plant leaves was a compound they named chlorophyll, from the Greek words for "greenish-yellow" and "leaf." Although they did not know it at the time, they had isolated the compound that makes photosynthesis possible.

Chlorophyll is made up of five elements: the four basic elements of life—carbon, oxygen, hydrogen, and nitrogen—plus a fifth, magnesium, a metallic element derived from soil that is essential to almost all living matter. Humans, for example, need to consume 200 milligrams of magnesium a day—by eating plants or animals that feed on plants—to maintain healthy bones and blood. It is the magnesium in chlorophyll that makes leaves and needles appear green; the molecule absorbs the red and blue components of sunlight, but not the green. When light is reflected off a plant, it is the unabsorbed green light we see; we live in a green world because our soil and plants contain magnesium.

Donald Culross Peattie, in his book *Flowering Earth*, recalls how, as a student of botany at Harvard, he learned to extract chlorophyll from the ivy leaves that grew on the outside of Harvard's venerable buildings. He and his fellow students first boiled the leaves, then placed them in alcohol; the leaves lost their color and the alcohol became green. They then diluted the alcohol with water and added benzol; the solution separated, with the yellowing alcohol on the bottom and the thick, green benzol floating on top like pond scum: "You could simply decant the latter carefully off into a test tube," Peattie writes, "and there you had chlorophyll extract, opaque, trembling, heavy, a little viscous and oily, and smelling, but much too rankly, like a lawn-mower's blades after a battle with rainy grass." Using spectrum analysis, Peattie learned that the constituents of a chlorophyll molecule were eerily familiar. "To me, a botanist's apprentice, a future naturalist," he writes, "there was just one fact to quicken the pulse. That fact is the close similarity between chlorophyll and hemoglobin, the essence of our blood." This is no fanciful comparison, but a literal, scientific analogy: "The one significant difference in the two structural formulas is this: that the hub of every hemoglobin molecule is one atom of iron, while in chlorophyll it is one atom of magnesium." Just as chlorophyll is green because magnesium absorbs all but the green light spectrum, blood is red because iron absorbs all but the red. Chlorophyll is green blood. It is designed to capture light; blood is designed to capture oxygen.

Within the spongy cells are numerous tiny packages, the chloroplasts, and inside each chloroplast are a number of smaller packages called grana. These are composed of alternating layers of chlorophyll and fatty proteins suspended in liquid enzymes and salts. Each chloroplast thus works as an amazingly efficient photovoltaic cell that captures the Sun's energy and uses it to turn air into food. Chloroplasts can capture nearly limitless sunlight for the energy required to turn carbon dioxide and water into sugar. With energy tied up in bonds of glucose, the sugar molecule could be stored and used at any future time to synthesize the building blocks of macromolecules: lipids, starch, proteins, and nucleic acids.

"How," Peattie asks, "does the chlorophyll, green old alchemist that it is, transmute the dross of earth into living tissue?" Water pulled up from the root enters the needle through the xylem attached to the stem and percolates out among the spongy cells. Carbon dioxide is drawn into the needle through the stomata. When a photon of sunlight hits a chloroplast, one electron is ejected from each molecule of chlorophyll; this energy excites the molecule which then uses that excitation to carry out a chemical reaction.

Actually, there is a series of split-second reactions; the energy released by the ejected electron separates water into its component parts, hydrogen and oxygen. Carbon dioxide is also torn apart into its separate elements. Then the released carbon, hydrogen, and oxygen recombine to form carbonic acid, which is instantly changed into formic acid—the same compound that gives ants their sting. This becomes formaldehyde and hydrogen peroxide, which immediately break down into water, oxygen, and glucose. Some of the glucose is then converted into fructose, or fruit sugar, for immediate use by the tree, and the rest is compressed into starch, which is sent down to the roots to be stored for future use. The oxygen and water vapor are ejected through the stomata by expiration and transpiration. Other products eventually formed by this process include amino acids—the essential ingredients of protein—and various fats and vitamins.

All this chemical activity requires light, and all the light is drawn from the Sun, which, although 150 million kilometers (93 million miles) away, delivers energy to Earth at the astounding rate of 215,000,000,000,000,000 calories per second. Most of this energy is never involved in photosynthesis—most of it falls on desert sands, mountain slopes, the polar ice caps, or our exposed skin. But enough—a mere 1 percent—is used by plants to keep the planet alive.

SALAMANDER BURNING BRIGHT

In the low, cool shade cast by our tree and its neighboring ferns, lupines, and fireweed, a western redback salamander (*Plethodon vehiculum*) pauses in her search for insects to scout the stream bank for predators or a potential mate. One of twenty-one species of salamanders found in the Douglas-fir's range, this western redback is a long, sleek, black female with a distinct copper-red brush stroke running down her back, along her tail, and over the upper sides of her legs. Her belly is pale, with white and black flecks, and as she waits in the darkness her ribs expand and contract like a bellows. The western redback is a lungless amphibian, which means she doesn't breathe through her mouth but absorbs oxygen directly through her skin. To accomplish this, the salamander has developed an epidermis so porous that it is in constant danger of dehydration, which is why it is found only in dark, damp microclimates. Its skin is as delicate and fragile as the lining of our lungs.

Other northern lungless salamanders, such as the clouded salamander (*Aneides ferreus*) and the ensatina (*Ensatina eschscholtzii*), prefer to spend their time at the centers of rotting logs on the floor of the old-growth forest, where there are plenty of springtails to eat and the humidity is constant, even during a fire. But the western redback is found more often in open areas, in clearings and burns, usually on western-facing talus slopes where the soil is gravelly and there is little direct sun, some low protective foliage, and access to water. All salamanders are poikilothermal, meaning that their body temperatures vary according to the temperature of the objects around them—air, stones, decaying matter. Western redbacks prefer it a little warmer than some other species.

This one has a very small range, only 2 square meters (22 square feet), and she doesn't seem to worry about protecting it— salamander density in this part of the forest is high, almost 800 per hectare (2.5 acres), and so a rigorous territorial defense policy would consume a lot of energy. For the most part, she keeps out of rotting logs, where she would likely encounter other salamanders, and when she does go into a log she stays close to the surface, just under the bark, rather than burrowing deep into the decaying heartwood. She seems to like cavities at the bases of sword ferns. April is her mating month, and in June she will deposit her eggs on land rather than in water, as aquatic salamanders do. Her young will emerge from the eggs looking like perfectly formed but diminutive replicas of herself.

Only forty species of salamanders are known worldwide, but they are widespread. At the time of our tree's ascendance, salamanders were known in Europe and Asia Minor and into Africa. There was even the legendary fire salamander (*Salamandra salamandra*). According to Aristotle, whose word was still law, fire salamanders were immune to flame; they were so cold-blooded they could put out fires merely by walking through them. Until the seventeenth century there were stories of people seeing salamanders resting calmly on burning logs in their fireplaces. They were also supposed to be extremely venomous. Alexander the Great reported that four thousand of his men and two thousand horses died instantly after drinking from a stream into which a single salamander had fallen. If a salamander climbed up the trunk of a tree, the fruit was poisoned. There may be a scientific basis for such myths, for certain salamanders secrete a thin, milklike substance that is a deadly neurotoxin when swallowed, which is why most predators leave them alone. It was thought that a cloak made from salamander skin was immune to fire, making it a handy garment for an alchemist or for someone wanting to pass for a magician. The Pope had one, for example. Alas, its reputation was false. Dioscorides tossed dozens of salamanders into a fire to see what would happen to them; they burned to crisps. Clearly, more careful observation was needed. Marco Polo, during his twenty-five-year sojourn in China, which began in 1271, looked for the creature without success. "Of the salamander under the form of a serpent supposed to exist in fire," he reported upon his return to Venice in 1296, "I could never discover any traces in the eastern regions."

Although he never saw a fire salamander, he did report on the production, in the region of Chinchitalas, of something called salamander cloth, made from "a substance procured from the mountain," which consisted of "fibers not unlike those of wool. This, after being exposed to the sun to dry, is pounded in a brass mortar, and is then washed until the earthy particles are separated." The resulting wool is then spun into thread and woven into cloth, which is placed in a fire for an hour until it turns white "and does not burn." He thought the mined substance might be fossil salamander skin. We know it as asbestos. "It is said that they preserve in Rome a napkin made from this material, sent as a gift from the Great Khan to the Pope to make a wrapper for the Holy Sudarium of Jesus Christ."

It is now known that salamanders' chromosomal cells are jammed with about a hundred times more chromosomal DNA than those of mammals, including human beings. No one knows what all those extra nucleotides are doing there; they may be simply copies of functioning DNA, what geneticists call junk DNA. But generally, as Aristotle observed, nothing in nature is superfluous. Salamanders are still a mystery.

THE WIND RISING from the ocean stirs the young broadleaf foliage along the streambed above our young tree. Later in its life, the tree will need defenses from the wind, which will rock and

A lungless salamander

buffet its crown, threaten to tear off its branches, weaken its grip in the soil, fan ground fires at its base, and blow its seeds high into the mountains. Windstorms rank second only to fire in determining the shape and makeup of the large forests; over the next five centuries, major storms with winds exceeding 200 kilometers (125 miles) per hour will blow down millions of hectares of Douglas-fir forest. For the present, though, the wind is a benign force.

THREE

G R O W T H

When first the unflowering Fern-forest,
Shadowed the dim lagoons of old,
A vague unconscious long unrest
Swayed the great fronds of green and gold.
AGNES MARY FRANCES ROBINSON, "Darwinism"

It has been sixteen years since the fire. The burn is no longer a black hole in the forest but a swath of fresh greenery, lower than the unburned portions but obviously returned to vitality. The smell of charcoal has long left the air. After an exceptionally wet spring, with more than 150 centimeters (60 inches) of rain, the summer has been hot and dry with vigorous forest growth. It is early fall now, and the stream is invisible from the ridge, although there is a sense of it—a line of glossy green—flowing among the dark trunks and writhing roots of the forest floor. The forest is still quiet, but it is not the silence of death, as after the fire, but rather the stillness of rest, of waiting.

Western redcedars and a few bigleaf and vine maples have grown in the burn and now form part of the forest community. For a short distance along the stream's banks, red alders (*Alnus rubra*), discernible as a darker, shinier stripe, wind through the needle forest. Mature, forty-year-old red alders can grow to 24 meters (80 feet) in the open, but like the Douglas-firs that now overshadow them, they are intolerant of shade and therefore, in this forest, will be short-lived. Long before they reach their full height, the older ones will die out, leaving the forest floor open and dark and somewhat monotonous. But for now, at ground level, their smooth, near-white trunks are like beams of muted light in the dim undergrowth. Wilson's warblers, solitary vireos, and, in winter, dark-eyed juncos find them a reliable source of insects, spiders, and seeds.

They're called red alder because there is a red pigment in their inner bark. Every year a Coast Salish family climbs up to the old burn and camps for one or two nights by the streambed. They call the red alder *yuhsáwi*. During the day they peel off its bark in triangular strips—being careful not to girdle the tree's stem and to leave the living cambium layer unscathed—roll the triangles into tight scrolls, and, when they break camp, carry them down to their coastal village. There they will pound the inner bark to release the color, mix it with fish oil, and use the mixture to decorate their redcedar-bark clothing and dog-hair blankets.

The coast people are conscious of living a life safely balanced between two nurturing zones, the sea before them and the forest behind. They are not so concerned about above and below, the sky and the Earth, but of the coast and the forest they are knowledgeable and experienced.

At night, in the red alder camp, the house leader teaches the names and properties of the trees. The bark of the western hemlock, *skwúpuhc*, makes a grayish brown paste with which the people dye their fishing nets, making them invisible to the salmon. The western redcedar, *xpáy'uhc*, they use for their canoes, longhouses, tools, and medicines. The large leaves of the bigleaf maple, *ê'ólhac*, make excellent berry baskets. Cottonwood leaves, *q'wuh*, are good for bandages because they stick to the skin when crushed. Douglas-fir, *êuhbídac*, is light but very strong, a fuel tree; its bark burns exceptionally well, though it sends out many sparks, and its green boughs are burned in sweat lodges to cleanse human minds and hearts. The house leader also tells stories—of the Flood Tree, *qwutl'uhc*, for example, the sacred madrone, or arbutus, in which the early people, adrift in their dugout canoe during the Great Flood, found shelter and were saved. All the stories connect the land and the sea, as do the people themselves.

THE *B*UDDING TREE

Our tree is 8 meters (25 feet) high and has sixteen tiers of branches radiating from its tapered stem; the bottom eight have dropped off. Its diameter at the base is 35 centimeters (14 inches). New shoots at the tips of the tree's branches are lighter in color than the mature needles, and there are new buds at their bases.

But there are no branches among the lower trees because the tree's growth is greatest where it will do the most good: higher up in full sunlight and below ground.

Like many other conifers, such as lodgepole and Ponderosa pines, where soil depth permits, the Douglas-fir sends down a deep central taproot to anchor the enormous superstructure that will eventually rise high above the ground. Evergreens also have a web of side roots that spread out to form the platform on which the tree rests. Some of the thicker lateral roots hump above the ground, like the backs of diving gray whales that come into the bays to feed on herring. Where these roots are exposed to sunlight, they distribute chlorophyll to the inner bark, which produces localized growth hormones that facilitate the transfer of nutrients up through the xylem. Where its lateral roots encounter those of a neighboring Douglas-fir, the two root stems will graft together, sometimes longitudinally, sometimes at right angles, to form a single vascular unit, and so each tree helps the other by sharing hormones and starches through their conjoined phloem.

A grove of trembling aspens has a different sort of association of roots. Aspen trunks are in fact clones growing from a single root system. This is an adaptation that has allowed a single organism to exploit different niches, from high, dry, sun-swept ground to low, wet valley bottoms and riverbanks, since through the roots aspens in poor soil can receive nourishment from aspens in rich soil. Such clonal aspen colonies achieve huge proportions covering massive areas. One, in the state of Utah, occupies 43 hectares (106 acres), with a total mass of more than 6,000 tonnes, nearly three times the mass of a single giant sequoia and one of the largest living organisms on the planet. What may be the largest single organism in the world is an *Armillaria ostoyae* fungus found in a mixed conifer forest in the Blue Mountains of northeast Oregon. It is 8,500 years old and covers nearly 10 square kilometers (4 square miles).

Our tree also benefits from the roots of other trees by means of its ectomycorrhizal fungal partnerships. Red alders, for example, are especially good at removing nitrogen from the air and fixing it in the soil—amounts up to 300 kilograms per hectare (more than 2,600 pounds per acre) per year have been recorded, enough to supply the forest for the next two hundred years—where it is broken down by bacteria and siphoned by fungi into the roots of other trees, including ours. In return, the red alder roots receive up to 10 percent of their stored starch from their neighbors. Through both its intraspecies and its interspecies association, our tree benefits from being part of the forest ecosystem and thus increases its own chances of survival. Despite the red alder's efficiency at fixing nitrogen, torrential rains on steep slopes and thin soil flushes much of the nitrogen into rivers and out to sea. In all forests, nitrogen concentration is often the factor limiting growth.

In early April, cells in the meristems along the tree's trunk and branches began to divide to form a new cambium layer pinched between the outer bark and the outer sapwood; this is how the tree grows, by adding a new layer of living cells atop the previous year's layer. The old cells die and become the outermost ring of heartwood, and the new sapwood assumes most of the task of water transfer. Every year the tree adds a new ring to its axes. The rings are slightly thicker at the base of the living crown than they are at the top, but there are more of them at the base of the tree. As a result, the tree's trunk is continually forming in the shape of a taper. The angle of taper is sharper in the crown, between the lowest branches and the top of the tree, than it is between the crown and the base.

In the spring, when the temperature rises above 5°C (41°F), cells in the meristems of the crown section produce auxins that promote cambial growth as they spread down the trunk at the rate of 5 to 10 centimeters (2 to 4 inches) per hour. Where buds have formed the previous years, auxins accumulate and the cells divide more rapidly to promote lateral or axillary growth that eventually becomes new branches. In mid-May, these buds flush, or burst open. Tiny needles, like paintbrushes dipped in green, emerge from the ends. Some of these buds develop into new shoots, but this year others will develop into cones, and the seventeen-month cycle of producing pollen, fertilizing eggs, and dispersing seeds is under way.

The buds that will become cones are located primarily near the top of the tree, in the year-old shoots. Some of them—those close to the base of the shoots—will become male, or pollen cones, while others, out nearer the shoot tips, will become female, or seed cones. It does not become clear until the middle of July which buds will develop into shoots and which will become cones. Until they are ten weeks old, all of them look as though they are going to form shoots, but gradually distinctions among the three types of bud growth—shoots, seed cones, and pollen cones—make themselves apparent. By fall, those destined to become shoots have initiated a spiral series of leaf primordia, future pollen cones display a spiral series of structures that look like emergent leaves but eventually become pollen sacs, and seed-cone buds develop spiral primordia that later develop into the mouse-tail bracts characteristic of Douglas-fir seed cones.

Now it is September and all three bud types appear to be dormant. Cell division is taking place within them, however, and throughout the winter some physiological activity will continue, although at a reduced rate. More winter activity will take place in the buds destined to become cones than in those waiting to become shoots, and more will take place in the female cones than in the males. Some of that activity will be fueled by photosynthesis. The tree will continue to photosynthesize, to top up its winter supply of starch, as long as the temperature remains above 5 or 6°C (41 to 43°F). But for the most part, it will sleep, relying on the energy stored in its sapwood and leaves during the summer to get it through the winter and to feed its initial kickoff in the spring. This process will be repeated every second year for the rest of our tree's long life.

BLOWING IN THE *Wind*

Although a conifer appears to grow straight up, like a post emerging from the ground, in fact it coils out of the earth, like a missile rifling through the air. The mathematical expression for this growth pattern is the "dynamic spiral," and it explains the tapering trunk and limbs and the arrowhead shape of its crown. Beneath the bark, the grain in the wood grows upward in a spiral. The shape of the trunk thus reflects the shape of the tree, since each is the result of logarithmic growth increase: new growth is added each year not only to the tree's girth but also to its height. This spiral pattern is repeated in many things in nature that grow by an increase in basal circumference as well as in overall length: the shells of most mollusks, the twisted tusks of narwhals and elephants, the overlapping pattern of petals around the center of a rose. It is also apparent in spiral galaxies throughout the solar system and in the double-helix coils of DNA bound up in human haploid cells. In a conifer, the spiral is also evident in the structure of the cone.

Although the external features and delivery systems may seem totally different, there is very little difference between plant sex and animal sex; both plants and animals combine genetic material from two parents to produce an offspring. In a conifer, the female cone carries the ovules, each of which contains an egg. When fertilized by a male gamete from the pollen cone, the egg becomes the seed, which is a tree in embryo plus a supply of nutrients.

Instead of petals, pine cones have scales arranged in a spiral around a central axis so that no single scale falls directly on top of another, and the whole complex can be sealed with wax and resin to shed water in the spring and retain water during drought in the summer and to await the proper autumn conditions for seed dispersal. The males, located at the bases of the branchlets, are the pollen cones. They are smaller than the seed cones and also develop more slowly, remaining enclosed in bud scales for most of the first year and over the winter, their cells quietly dividing to form five-celled grains that in February begin to mature within each pollen sac. The cones open just before their pollen is due for release in the spring. They are pollinizers in waiting, like drones in a beehive, apparently dozing until they are called upon to serve the female and then die, which they do once their duty is performed. Each male cone consists of a central axis and scales; at the base of each scale are two pollen sacs. The male cones are more abundant on the lower branches, and the seed cones are higher up, so that when pollen is released from male cones in April it is less likely to fertilize the seed cones of the same tree. Instead, the pollen will be picked up by the wind and blown to the female cones of a neighboring tree.

The female cones are much more complicated than the male cones. Their growth, which begins in February, is the result of the elongation of the central axis as well as the enlargement of the bud scales. At this point the seed cones are arranged horizontally on the branch, but since growth is more rapid on the bottom half of the cone, where more auxins accumulate, the cones will bend upward and by the time of bud burst, in April, will be standing erect. At the base of each bract is a scale, and attached to the base of each scale are two ovules. At the central axis end of the ovule is a tiny opening, or micropyle, through which the young root will eventually emerge; soon pollen grains from the male cone will enter through this opening and begin their journey to fertilization.

The male cones begin to enlarge in March, when the pollen grains are fully developed. As their axes lengthen, the new growth pushes open the bud scales and, during bud burst in April, pollen is released from its sequestered sacs. The air is saturated with pollen rain. The female cones, now standing erect on the branches, their bracts spread wide like so many tiny open umbrellas, are in a perfect position to receive the sheets of dustlike pollen grains being borne to them on the wind.

Pollination by wind is a wild but dubious adventure and is considered quite primitive among plants, since there is no control over where the pollen will land. In contrast, pollination carried out by an insect provides a reasonable probability that pollen stuck to the insect will find its way to another flower of the same species. In fact, many species evolve flowers that are attractive to specific insects for just that purpose. But conifers developed their pollinating techniques before there were flying insects. The flowering plants, or angiosperms, evolved only during the Cretaceous period, which ended 65 million years ago, when gymnosperms—conifers, cycads, and ginkgos—had already been around for at least 300 million years.

There was not much in the way of pollen dispersal mechanisms to choose from in the Permian period, when trees began to distinguish themselves from ferns. There was water, but water was down on the ground. There were land animals, but they too were stuck on the ground. The sex organs of trees were well up in the air, and what else was up there but wind, which could carry a tree's pollen grains anywhere or nowhere? The trees that prospered were those that produced pollen grains so small and separate from one another that they would float on the slightest breeze and dispersed so many that the chances that some of them would fall on the female cone of another tree were significantly greater than zero. Wind-pollinated plants in general produce astronomical amounts of pollen, creating a fine mist in the air and coating the surface of mountain lakes. Flowering trees such as birch and hazel, which also rely on wind, produce up to 5 million pollen grains per catkin, and there are thousands of catkins on each tree. It's the shotgun approach to sex, but it seems to work.

It is certainly better than self-pollination, an option chosen by some later plants—most modern annual weeds, for example. Darwin noted that "nature . . . abhors perpetual self-pollination," perhaps because he recognized that, as with inbreeding in animals, self-pollination over time weakens the species. Abhoring self-pollination was not just a Victorian conceit; most human cultures have had taboos against inbreeding, especially primary brother-sister or parent-offspring incest, and some—precontact Inuit culture, for example—prohibited marriages all the way down to sixth cousins. Although many social mores lack a scientifically credible explanation or basis, there are good genetic justifications for this social taboo.

Red-backed vole and fir cones

Organisms that reproduce sexually carry two sets of chromosomes, one set from the male parent and the other from the female parent. Such an organism is referred to as a diploid; the one set of chromosomes carried in each sperm and egg is called haploid. Each chromosome carries hundreds of genes, which are arranged along the chromosome like beads on a string. These genes are also carried by the other, corresponding (homologous) chromosome. The genes at the same position on homologous chromosomes are referred to as alleles of each other and may be identical or different. For example, there are two different forms of a gene controlling the color of seeds in peas, one determining a yellow seed, the other green. In any pea plant, both alleles might be for yellow or for green, or one might be yellow, the other green. A plant carrying one gene for yellow and one for green has yellow seeds, so we say the gene for yellow is dominant to the gene for green, and the gene for green is recessive to the gene for yellow. Like other animals, every human being carries recessive alleles of genes which, if present in two copies, would result in death, malformations, or other defective traits. When people who are not related have children, the chance that they will carry the same recessive alleles for any trait may be very low. However, the more closely related a pair is, the greater the chance that both will carry the same recessive alleles, and in a highly incestuous line, the odds jump astronomically—from 1 in 10,000, for some genetically inherited diseases, to 1 in 20. Continual inbreeding, generation after generation, increases the odds again and soon creates a group in which the chance of inheriting the recessive trait may be as great as that of being born without it. If the particular inherited variation makes individuals less fit to survive in their environment, it leads to extinction; if it makes them fitter to adapt to a new or changed environment, it is beneficial, and bestows an even greater selective advantage. But Darwin noticed that perpetual inbreeding seldom led to beneficial adaptations.

At one time it was thought that organisms that were especially well adapted to a specific environment would displace all others and eventually weed out other genes that did not confer a high survival rate—in other words, that individuals would tend to become more and more genetically similar, or homogeneous. During the 1960s, as sophisticated molecular techniques were developed, geneticists began to look at the products of specific genes in individual organisms—fruit flies, for example—expecting to find that most of their genes were homogeneous. To their surprise, the opposite proved to be true; when specific genes were examined, a profusion of different allelic forms was found. This diversity is now called genetic polymorphism, and it has become the very definition of a healthy, well-adapted species. Populations of organisms such as Bengal tigers or pandas, when reduced to a small number of individuals, do not have enough genetic diversity to ensure the health of the species—eventually, all the members of the species will be genetically related and so all breeding will be inbreeding.

In species with a large number of individuals concentrated in a confined area, such as an island or a very small ecological niche, maintaining genetic polymorphism may seem counterintuitive: why select for lots of diversity rather than focus on the best combination of alleles for the given environment? That might work if environmental conditions never changed, but over geological timescales, change is the norm. The Sun is now almost 30 percent warmer than it was when life first arose; mountain ranges have appeared and worn down; oceans have filled and emptied; ice ages have come and gone. Yet all the while life has survived and even flourished. Genetic polymorphism ensures that there is always a heterogeneous pot of genes within a given species that will provide a variety of combinations, some of which might be better suited to the changing conditions than were those of the parents.

Diversity offers resilience and adaptability. Nature appears to be built upon a series of nested differences. There is individual gene diversity within each species, many different kinds of species within habitats, habitat variety within ecosystems, and a great array of different ecosystems around the planet. This is the diversity that has given life its resilience within the biosphere. As anthropologist Wade Davis points out, there is another sphere in which diversity is equally important for adaptive survival: the human sphere. Human cultures around the world—from Inuit in the Arctic to Kayapo in the Amazon basin to Aborigines in Australia and the !San in the Kalahari Desert—have all, over hundreds of generations, accumulated knowledge that has enabled them to flourish within an amazingly diverse set of environments. Each base of knowledge is deeply rooted in an understanding of place, which we might call home. Taking all those cultures together, the knowledge they contain makes up the ethnosphere, the sum of all the ways in which human beings have imagined the world, how it works and where we belong in it. Just as all the levels of biological diversity in the biosphere are crucial for life's persistence on Earth, so diversity within the ethnosphere ensures a continuing body of shared knowledge that has been critical for our survival as a species in an astounding variety of ecosystems.

Monoculture, the spreading of a single species or genetic strain over a wide area to the exclusion of other strains or species, is the antithesis of diversity and makes a species or an ecosystem vulnerable to changing climatic conditions, predators, pests, or diseases—as we have learned at great cost through the experience of agriculture, fisheries, and forestry. A Douglas-fir forest cannot be planted with individuals selected, or genetically manipulated in a laboratory, for growth rate, size, and wood quality without regard to the trees' surroundings and the other species with which they have evolved in association. Biologist E.O. Wilson foresees a time in the not-too-distant future when all harvestable trees will be grown on "tree farms," just as all edible salmon will be from fish farms, chickens from poultry farms, and so on. The consequent loss of genetic polymorphism and species diversity will render the entire genetic structure of the planet vulnerable to unpredictable and uncontrollable forces. This almost happened when vast acreages of one commercial variety of hybrid corn were grown across the southern United States in the 1970s. The appearance of a mutant fungal disease wiped out hundreds of thousands of hectares in a matter of months.

Wind dispersal may be primitive, but it still allows the perpetuation of genetic polymorphism, and it has advantages over some other methods of outbreeding, such as dispersal by mammals or birds. First, there is almost always wind over a forest. At higher elevations, where the spring weather is usually cool and wet, the chances are greater that there will be few mammals or birds around in April than that there will be no wind. A second advantage is that the tree need not expend a great deal of energy making its sex organs attractive to pollinating insects. Those large, showy displays on flowering plants are expensive to create and require energy to maintain. A cone is a comparatively low-maintenance organ. It lasts longer than a flower because it is made of more durable materials, and it does not have to be constantly refilled with sugary rewards for visiting insects. A third advantage is distance: wind-borne pollen has been found up to 5,000 kilometers (3,100 miles) from the nearest plant that could have produced it, much farther than any bee, mosquito, or passing animal is likely to take it. This dispersal increases genetic diversity as well as the chance that the female cones of even the loneliest of pines will be pollinated and produce seeds. It should also serve as a warning to proponents of genetically engineered organisms who maintain that such crops can be contained.

Douglas-fir pollen grains are more packed with stored food than those of most other conifers and so, being larger and heavier, do not disperse quite that far, but in a forest composed predominantly of Douglas-firs they do not need to. Researchers counting pollen grains on the ground several kilometers from the nearest Douglas-fir have found an average of 123 grains per square centimeter (794 grains per square inch); three-quarters of a kilometer (half a mile) from the nearest Douglas-fir, the figure rose to 320 grains per square centimeter (2,000 grains per square inch); and immediately under a Douglas-fir, there were 800 grains per square centimeter (5,161 grains per square inch). The most effective distance for wind pollination, they determined, was up to ten times the tree's height, which for our tree means that its pollen falls most effectively on trees within 100 meters (330 feet) of it. This area embraces most trees within the old burn and a few older trees on the burn's edge.

PLANTS IN THE $\mathcal{R}$ENAISSANCE

At the end of the Middle Ages, when our tree was beginning its fifteenth year of life, the world in general was becoming more aware of plants. In architecture, wooden beams replaced stone arches in larger buildings, such as cathedrals, in which semicircular wooden centerings enabled high, vaulted ceilings to be built over unsupported naves. In clothing, wool and leather were challenged by lighter, cheaper, and more fashionable materials made from plants. When Columbus arrived in the West Indies in 1492, he was offered not gold but fruit and vegetables and skeins of cotton yarn for barter by the Taino people—one of the reasons he thought he had reached the East Indies—and six years later, Vasco da Gama returned from his voyage to India with bolts of spun cotton from Calicut. Many of the voyages of exploration during the next two centuries were inspired by the need for new sources of cotton fiber. And by the end of the fifteenth century, linen paper, made from flax and imported into Europe from China (where it had been in use since the first century), had all but replaced vellum or parchment in book production, having proved its durability. This was where plants had their most significant impact on the new social order, because they made possible the rapid spread of printing.

When Johannes Gutenberg invented the printing press in Mainz, Germany, between 1447 and 1455, the ready availability of linen paper allowed books to be printed quickly and inexpensively. A single copy of the Gutenberg Bible, for example, handwritten by a monk on parchment instead of printed on linen paper, would have taken twenty years to produce and required the skins of two hundred sheep.

Gutenberg's genius was in capitalizing on the huge demand for texts created by expanded enrollment in the universities, which in turn resulted from the rediscovery of texts by the ancient Greek and Arabic natural philosophers. His invention paved the way for the mass production of books. Presses began cranking out new editions of Aristotle, Euclid, Dioscorides, and Theophrastus, so wider discussion of the implications and shortcomings of these classical authors was not only possible but inevitable. Reading, and soon education, became the passion of the masses rather than the pastime of the rich. The new thirst for knowledge was reflected in the extraordinary speed with which printing spread throughout Europe. Within fifty years of the Gutenberg Bible there were printing presses in sixty cities in Germany and others in Italy, Spain, Hungary, Denmark, Sweden, and England, all busily producing books for public consumption. It is estimated that by the end of the fifteenth century more than 20 million books had been printed; with an average print run of less than five hundred copies, more than forty thousand titles were placed in the avid hands of ordinary readers.

A good many of those new titles were about plants. The *Latin Herbarius* was printed in 1484, followed by the *German Herbarius* in 1485, and although both were compendiums of plants described by classical authors, usually Dioscorides, for the first time they also contained addenda with descriptions of plants found locally. The number of plants known to science increased quickly and dramatically, especially after Columbus returned from the New World with specimens that bore no resemblance to anything described by the Greeks or even by Marco Polo. The effect of this deluge of new plants on fifteenth-century botany was similar to the effect of the invention of the telescope on sixteenth-century astronomy. Eyes opened. A new way of thinking about the world was unavoidable, a turning of the head from perpetually looking over the shoulder to gazing more certainly at the present and even peering into the future.

On May 10, 1534, Jacques Cartier's two ships "came to the new found land." Over the next few weeks, sailing in the Gulf of St. Lawrence, Cartier encountered numerous small islands populated by strange plants, animals, and birds. Most of the land, he reported, was barren, "not to be called the new land, but rather stones, and wilde furres, and a place for wilde beastes, for in all the North Island I didde not see a Cartloade of good earth." On an island he named White Sands he saw "nothing else but Mosse, and small Thornes scattered here and there, withered and drye." One group of islands, however, where they stopped for water and wood, was fertile enough to support vegetation, and Cartier took delight in describing their bounty. "They have the best soyle that ever we saw, for that one of their fields is more worth, than all the new land. We found it all full of goodly trees, medowes, champaines full of wild peason blomes, as thicke, as ranke, and as faire, as any can be seene in Brittayne, that they seemed to have bin plowed and sowed. There was also great store of gooseberies, strawberries, damaske roses, parseley, with other very sweete and pleasant hearbes." A pity Cartier had no botanist on board, as later expeditions were to have. His "wild peason" could have been any native member of the Leguminosae, from the beach pea (*Lathyrus japonicus*) to purple vetch (*Vica americana*), and was assuredly unknown in Brittayne. And whichever of the dozen members of the rose family he saw, it was certainly not a damask.

New plants required new names, and these were increasingly given in the vernacular, rather than in Greek or Latin. The plants were drawn and described by professional herbalists and—a new kind of person—amateur botanists. Such was the German botanist Jerome Bock, whose *Neu Kreütterbuch*, published in 1539, was a record of the plants Bock observed on his field trips and to which he gave German names. He organized the seven hundred plants he described and illustrated into Theophrastus's three categories—herbs, shrubs, and trees—but also described their physical characteristics, such as height, foliage, type of root system, and time of flowering, and arranged them not alphabetically or medicinally but by similarity of form, corolla shape, color, and formation of their seed capsules. It was like an early *Peterson's Guide to the Plants of Germany*, and it earned Bock the title of father of German botany.

The rising interest in exotic plants in turn led to another new phenomenon, the public botanical garden. Monasteries, convents, universities, and royal houses had long kept private "physic" gardens, walled enclosures or even large plantations in which plants were raised for food or for their medicinal value, were studied and used for demonstration purposes in lectures, or were simply maintained as beautiful, healthy places to which the privileged could repair when fatigued by the increasingly crowded and plague-ridden cities. The new botanical gardens featured plants from around the world and displayed them for their beauty and interest as much as for their usefulness. The famous Boboli Gardens in Florence were begun in 1550, when Cosimo I de' Medici bought and expanded the Pitti Palace. Designed by Niccolò Pericoli, the gardens comprised 320 hectares (almost 800 acres) of the known world's most luscious and exotic plants, arranged for the exclusive enjoyment of the Medici family. By this time, the first public botanical garden had opened in Padua, in 1545, under the direction of Luigi Anguillara. In 1567 the Botanical Gardens of Bologna were established by Ullise Aldrovandi, who was also the first professor to include, in his lectures on natural history at the University of Bologna, plants that were of no known medicinal value and so valued merely because they existed.

Perhaps the most influential botanist of the time was the Italian Prospero Alpini, who was born in 1553 and was therefore almost exactly contemporary with Shakespeare. He studied medicine at the University of Padua, knew the botanical gardens there intimately, and later traveled to Egypt, lived in Cairo for three years, and then returned to the University of Venice to become a *lettore dei semplici*. His *De Plantis Aegypti*, published in 1592, introduced a host of exotic plants to his curious readers, including many that would have a profound effect on the future of European commerce, such as the banana tree (*Musa sapientum*) and the coffee bush (*Coffea arabica*). The coffee and bananas now grown so prolifically in South America both come from trees originally planted there by European merchants who brought them from Africa. Although he didn't know the exact mechanism, Alpini also observed that the fertilization of a tree, in this case the date palm (*Phoenix dactylifera*), was a sexual process, thereby corroborating the beliefs of the Assyrians, who, 4,000 years earlier, had performed elaborate rituals in which priests cross-fertilized date palms. Gardeners had been pollinating and cross-pollinating plants for centuries, and Alpini was among the first botanists to investigate how pollination occurred. He described the phototropic movement of leaves of the tamarind tree (*Tamarindus indica*) without realizing that their movement followed that of the Sun— he thought they might be gasping for air. His interest in plants was neither mystical nor academic; he looked upon them with wonder and curiosity, which is to say with the eyes of a scientist rather than those of a magician or herbalist. Both Alpini and Shakespeare died in 1616. When that other Prospero, the hero of *The Tempest*, Shakespeare's final play, laid aside his book of incantations, the age of magic was over.

A WORLD OF FERNS

The fan of slender sword ferns (*Polystichum scopulinum*) is still growing at the base of our tree, although the salamander has moved on. There is something elemental about ferns; their beauty is a mathematical beauty, like that of snowflakes or crystals. They look like a plant designed by a computer programmed to illustrate chaos theory. They have the same basic structure as our tree, but in only two dimensions. Whereas the branches of a tree radiate in all directions from the central stem, sword fern fronds are paired and flat, like the shadow of a tree. Like all ferns, the sword fern is a lacy, elegant plant, each leaf in the swirl rising on its vascular tissue to a height of a meter and a half (5 feet), with 30-centimeter-long (12-inch-long) pale green fingers spreading from the axis like knife blades, arranged evenly on either side and tapering toward the top, in the classic pattern. The fern's base, just above the buried, hiltlike rhizome, is covered with crisp brown scales.

Ferns grow abundantly in almost every habitat on Earth. The sword fern is one of dozens of members of the group, which also includes horsetails and club mosses, associated with the Douglas-fir forest understory, where the presence of ferns and salamanders is a sign of a healthy ecosystem. The deer fern (*Blechnum spicant*), the only member of its tropical genus found in North America, resembles the sword fern but is shorter, and its fronds are continuous rather than separate, more like a mower blade than a stack of knives; it grows in swampy areas where western redcedars are more at home. The sword and deer ferns are evergreens, but the oak fern (*Gymnocarpium dryopteris*) drops its triple-headed fronds in the fall; it prefers the acidic soils found on slopes and ledges. The licorice fern (*Polypodium glycyrrhiza*) is an epiphyte; it grows on the mossy trunks of the bigleaf maples.

Ferns look like primitive trees because that is exactly what they are. When marine plants, the algal seaweeds, moved onto land, they evolved into bryophytes (mosses and liverworts) and then, as the competition for light became fiercer, rose higher from the ground and became pteridophytes (plants with roots, stems, and leaves but no flowers or seeds). Horsetails were the most successful; the several species in our forest include field horsetails, water horsetails, smooth horsetails, and the various scouringrushes, so called because they look like bottle brushes and, in fact, when ground up, were used by Native people for scouring cooking utensils. Their stems contain silica as well as cellulose as a stiffening agent. Horsetail leaves are more like modified bud scales. Their stems are hollow and jointed, not unlike bamboo, and tough as nails; they will push aside concrete slabs and grow through asphalt.

For many millions of years, ferns, horsetails, and club mosses dominated the vegetative world, peaking during the Carboniferous period, when they grew with stems as thick as trees and shaded the swampy landmasses with their huge fronds. At the end of the

Carboniferous, however, when the climate became increasingly dry, the ferns died off en masse; the huge coal and oil deposits from the Carboniferous, which we have been exploiting for two centuries, are made up entirely of fossil pteridophytes. Club mosses are now tiny plants, but in the mid-nineteenth century, a fossil club moss from the Carboniferous was exposed in England's Bensham Coal seam that was so startlingly huge that the colliery called in scientists to examine it. Its trunk, before the branches started, was 12 meters (39 feet) long and 1 meter (3 feet) across at the base. No one had seen anything like it before, and few have since. It was broken up and sold as coal—it may even have fueled the locomotive pulling the train that brought the scientists back to Oxford—but the point had been made. The heat energy released whenever a lump of coal is burned was gathered from the Sun and stored 300 million years ago by a pteridophyte.

Ferns are cryptogams (from the Greek words for "hidden" and "wedlock"); they reproduce by means of spores, which were the first improvement over cell division as a means of reproduction. Spores seem to be a kind of transitional phase between cell division and blatant sex. Ferns reproduce by the alternation of generations, a phenomenon first described in 1851 by German botanist Wilhelm Hofmeister, whose interest in cell division and pollen formation perhaps arose from the fact that he suffered from severe myopia; he had a penchant for examining everything close up. He became adept at using a dissecting microscope and was the first botanist to observe chromosomes within a cell nucleus, although he had no idea what they were.

The mature fern disperses thousands of spores. Those that fall on moist, shaded ground immediately begin to grow, but not into

Douglas-fir forest

discernible ferns; they grow into low, flat plants called gameto-phytes, a few centimeters in diameter, bearing on the undersurface of their leaves organs that produce not spores but the normal plant sex organs—the male antheridea and the female archegonia—more typical of those now found on conifers. These "hidden" sex organs "wed" to produce a seed that, when fertilized, grows into a fern. This complicated and indirect method of reproducing may have arisen to ensure a fall-back position for the family if climatic conditions suddenly became unfavorable to either strategy, spore production or seed dispersal.

Although climatic conditions changed drastically at the end of the Carboniferous and the huge plants died out, the fern family line has continued virtually unbroken to the present, which is why we have ferns in such numbers today. There are, worldwide, more than twenty thousand species of them, including at least one living fossil, the field horsetail, smaller than its ancestral monsters but one of the most widely dispersed of its kind. Some modern ferns are not so small: the beautiful tree ferns of the tropics often reach heights of 30 meters (100 feet) or more, and the giant horsetail (*Equisetum giganteum*) grows to 10 meters (33 feet). Most, how-ever, are under 1 meter (3 feet), having returned to the size of their forebears before the Carboniferous period. Fungi still reproduce solely by means of spores; gymnosperms, like our tree, all of which are descended from ferns, went the seed-producing route. Hofmeister showed conclusively that conifers were the evolution-ary link between ferns and the flowering plants.

Gymnosperm means "naked seed," from the Latin *gymno*, "naked" (Roman athletes performed naked in gymnasiums) and *sperma*, "seed." (Sperm whales are so called because it was once thought that the white, fatty substance in the whale's head was semen.) In the gymnosperms, the ovules within which the seeds develop lie openly on the cone scales, not covered by protective carpels as they are in the later flowering plants, or angiosperms ("enclosed seeds"). The seed-producing organs in conifers are still called sporophytes, a term held over from the spore-producing organs of ferns. And in the horsetails and club mosses, the spores are contained in strobili, Latin for "cones."

Gymnosperms evolved from ferns by getting a cambium. They also improved the strength of their stems, increased the amount of cellulose and lignin as stiffening agents, and filled the hollow centers with dead wood. Why they did so is a matter of speculation. Their adaptation may have been in response to the dry climate that followed the Carboniferous period; tough outer bark and a more efficient way of getting water from the roots into a lofty canopy would have been distinct evolutionary advantages. And developing elaborate root systems would have been a better way than relying on rhizomes for gathering increasingly scarce ground water. Or the strategy may have been a direct result of switching from spores to seed reproduction: as the seed and pollen cones became bigger and heavier, stronger stems were needed to support them. Cycads—palmlike tropical trees—for example, have gigantic reproductive organs. Whereas Douglas-fir ovules are measured in millimeters, those of some cycads are 6 centimeters (2 inches) long, and the cones that carry them can weigh up to 45 kilograms (100 pounds). Not even the treelike Carboniferous horsetails would have been able to hold up hundreds of cones of such collossal weight with their weak, hollow stems and lack of branches. Heartwood was the answer.

Coniferous trees have retained the slender shape of their fern ancestors, however; their trunks are tall and tapered, but they are not massive. Huge as a Douglas-fir might seem, it is proportionally one of the slimmest of the world's trees for its height. The flagpole at England's Kew Gardens was trimmed from a 371-year-old Douglas-fir that was 82 meters (270 feet) in height and only 82 centimeters (32 inches) across at the base. Shrink those dimensions down mathematically, and you get a tree fern.

SEX IN THE FOREST

The female cone of the Douglas-fir remains receptive to male pollen grains for twenty days, until about the end of April. Once a pollen grain has slipped down the smooth surface of the seed-cone bracts, it becomes enmeshed in the small, sticky hairs at the tip of the female ovule. For two months it luxuriates on this pubic patch while the ovule's labia swell around it; slowly the ovule engulfs the grain, which sinks into it like a croquet ball into a soft, silken pillow. By early May, an opening develops and the ovule becomes a vulva; the sticky hairs contract into the secret entrance to a passage called the micropylar canal, and the pollen grain is drawn in with them to begin its ascent toward the ovule's nucellus, or the part of the ovule that encloses the female gametophyte. As the pollen grain travels, it becomes elongated into a stiff rod, the walls of which are composed of cellulose and pectin. At this point the grain within the rod germinates and produces two gametes, or male sperm cells, and only then does the tube come into contact with the nucellus. The leading tip of the pollen tube meets, gently nudges, and finally penetrates the nucellus.

In pines, the pollen tube floats to the nucellus in a sweet, pearly fluid, called a pollination drop, inside the ovule, but Douglas-firs have no such fluid; pollen is moved along by a kind of muscular folding from the tip of the stigma to the nucellus. However, it is May in the coastal zone, which means rain, and some rainwater may get into the ovule. When that happens, the mechanism switches to one more like that of pines, and water eases the grain along the ovular canal to the nucellus, which then separates the water molecules and receives the germinated pollen. Over thousands of years, Douglas-fir has adapted to the probability of rain during bud burst, and pollination occurs without mishap either with or without its lubricating presence.

After penetrating the nucellus's surface tissue, the pollen tube rests for up to three weeks before continuing its journey to the neck of the ovule's archegonium, which it then enters, continuing its approach to the egg. At this point the total contents of the tube—the cytoplasm containing the nucleus, the body cell enclosing the two male gametes, and the stalk cell—coalesce into the shape of a cylinder and travel to the leading point of the pollen tube. The membrane separating the sperm cells from the cytoplasm ruptures, and the cells are ejaculated out of the pollen tube to fuse with the egg.

A female cone might receive more than one pollen grain. Any extra pollen grains dissolve and contribute to the seed's nutrient store.

UPON THE COMPLETION of the new botanical gardens in Paris, the Jardin des Plantes in the Faubourg Saint-Victor, in the summer of 1633, Guy de La Brosse was appointed its first director. He had been lobbying for such an establishment for the previous ten years, conceiving it primarily as a public garden but also as a laboratory for producing herbal medicines and as a teaching establishment for the new science of chemistry. In his first year as director,

La Brosse grew fifteen hundred plants and taught his students the characteristics of their "exteriors," by which he meant their forms and relationships, as well as of their "interiors," their pharmaceutical properties.

One of the most forward-looking scientists of his day, La Brosse was astounded by the degree to which plants functioned like animals. Both, he reasoned, have generation, growth, and movement and require nutrition, sleep (hibernation), and even sex; he was the first to suggest that plants reproduced, like animals, by the sexual mating of males and females. He even went so far as to wonder whether plants had souls. Life was life, he held, whether it was manifested in vegetable or animal form, and both life and death were regulated not by some seed planted in it at the time of its creation but by other factors contributed by the environment. In his new laboratory, he tried growing plants in pots containing sterilized soil and watering them with distilled water; when they died, he concluded that plants derived nutrients from soil in the form of salts and from water in the form of "manna." He also tried growing plants in a vacuum, with similar results; air, which he called *esprit*, was as necessary to plants as it was to animals. Plants did not have lungs, but neither did insects, and insects could not live without air. In a chapter on plant chemistry he came close to an understanding of photosynthesis; chemical change, he wrote, was the coming together of two agents—the plant's form, which he called "the Artisan," and fire, "the universal instrument," or "the Great Artist."

When his institution finally opened to the public in 1640, it contained eighteen hundred plants, many of which La Brosse had had sent from the East Indies and the Americas. Unfortunately, after so much preparation and anticipation, he died the following year.

His work, however, was continued by Rudolph Jakob Camerarius, a German physician who, in 1688, at the age of twenty-
three, was both extraordinary professor of medicine at the
University of Tübingen and director of the city's botanical gardens. He became interested in the question of plant sexuality in
1691, when, in the gardens, he observed a female mulberry tree
bearing plentiful fruit even though there were no male trees in the
vicinity. Upon examining the berries, he found that they contained
only abortive or empty seeds. He likened these seedless berries to
the unfertilized "wind eggs" of chickens and concluded that, like
hens, female trees needed male trees to produce viable seeds. So
far, however, this conclusion was merely an untested hypothesis
based on a single observation; Camerarius's contribution to the
science of botany was that he proceeded to test this hypothesis by
a series of experiments.

He set two female *Mercurialis annua* plants in pots indoors,
away from male plants, and allowed them to grow. Like the mulberry bush, the plants grew well and produced abundant berries,
but when the fruit was only half ripe it shriveled up and fell off,
containing no perfect seeds. He then removed the male inflores-
cences below the opening of the anthers from the male flowers of
Ricinus communis; the plant produced only "empty vessels, which
fell to the ground exhausted and dried up." He repeated the experiment with spinach, corn, and *Cannabis sativa*—marijuana—none
of which produced viable seeds. "It appears, therefore," he wrote
in *De sexu plantarum,* "justifiable to give these apices [the anthers]
a nobler name and to ascribe to them the significance of male sexual organs, since they are the receptacles in which the seed itself,
that is the powder which is the most subtle part of the plant, is

secreted and collected, to be afterwards supplied from them. It is equally evident, that the ovary with its style represents the female sexual organ in the plant."

IN EARLY JUNE, the female's egg nucleus swells and moves to the center of the archegonium, and the cytoplasm surrounding it becomes a dense and fibrous liquid. The nucleus, like an island at the center of a viscid lake, is the goal of the male gametes. As the pollen tube enters the nucellus, it spills its entire contents into the archegonium—the nuclei, both gametes (only one of which will reach the island), and stalk cell. The larger of the two gametes charges through the cytoplasm toward the egg nucleus at the center of the lake; the smaller gamete soon gives up and disintegrates, adding its generative material to the newly forming seed. The successful gamete reaches the nucleus, gradually penetrates its cell wall, and fertilizes the egg. By the second week in June, our tree has reached its sexual maturity. Within the developing embryos, cells continue to multiply throughout July and August, about the time the Pilgrim Fathers are tending their first crops in fields they found already cleared and vacated in the New England forest. By September, when the weather is favorable, the seeds on both coasts of North America are ready; in our tree, the female cone spreads its bracts and releases its forty thousand winged seeds into the warm, dry, autumn air.

M A T U R I T Y

As buds give rise by growth to fresh buds,
and these, if vigorous, branch out and overtop on all sides
many a feebler branch, so by generation I believe it has
been with the great Tree of Life, which fills with its dead and broken
branches the crust of the earth, and covers the surface with
its ever-branching and beautiful ramifications.

CHARLES DARWIN, *The Origin of Species*

For three hundred years our tree has been releasing its seeds to the warm September winds. In a good year, as this one is, it will produce a massive crop, but not every year has been a good year. Some autumns it released no seeds at all. All seed-producing trees have reproductive cycles—oaks are well known for their irregular bounty, but even domesticated apple trees produce well only every second year. The rhythm of a Douglas-fir's seed production has three intersecting cycles: its own two-year cycle; a seven-year cycle, for reasons that are still not known; and a twenty-two-year cycle that seems to mirror the peaks of sunspot activity on the Sun's surface. When these three curves coincide, which they do about once every ten years, the tree produces a bumper crop. If our tree were an oak, this year would be called a mast year.

Masting in oak trees has been linked to the appearance of Lyme disease through a complex chain of events. In 1975, medical scientists at Yale University investigated a cluster of more than fifty-one cases of juvenile arthritis in the small coastal town of Lyme, Connecticut. Allen Steele and his colleagues found the characteristic bull's-eye rash, called erythema migrans, and swollen joints that were the symptoms of what came to be called Lyme disease. The disease was shown to be caused by a spirochete, *Borrelia burgdorferi,* that had been discovered in the fluid of ticks by Willy Burgdorfer in 1982.

White-tailed deer normally feed on woody browse most of the time, but in mast years they spend their time in oak forests gorging on acorns. There they are attractive targets of adult deer ticks (*Ixodes scapularis*). The female ticks feed for four to five days when, engorged with blood, they fall off their host and overwinter in the leaf litter. In the spring, the female lays egg masses containing from several hundred to a few thousand eggs.

The huge numbers of acorns in the mast year also attract white-footed mice (*Peromyscus leucopus*), which gather and store large quantities of the nuts. They then have larger litters than normal and a higher survival rate of the young, with the result that in the year following a mast, the mouse population explodes, thereby providing lots of feeding opportunities to the newly hatched deer ticks. The white-footed mice are the reservoir of the spirochetes and, when they are parasitized by the baby ticks, transfer the bacteria with the blood meal and infect the ticks. Sated, the ticks drop to the forest floor to overwinter, emerging the next spring as nymphs, ready to spread the spirochetes. If a hiker chances by, the ticks will attach themselves to the unwitting victim. So two years after a masting event, a peak of Lyme disease in humans occurs.

Another fascinating aspect of masting was discovered by Lisa Curran and her coworkers, who studied Dipterocarpaceae, the main family of canopy forest trees found in Indonesia. From 1985 to 1999, the scientists focused on a 147-square-kilometer (57-square-mile) area of Gunung Palung National Park in Borneo. They discovered that the entire forest ecosystem had a masting phenomenon whereby over fifty dipterocarp tree species reproduced synchronously, producing massive crops of fruit and seeds in brief, intense periods in a cycle of about 3.7 years. When these bumper crops occur, the forest floor is littered with seeds and fruit. During a six-week masting interval, 93 percent of the trees drop their seeds, which, the researchers found, yielded up to 1300 kilograms per hectare (more than 5 tons per acre). Huge numbers of animals are attracted, including wild boar, orangutans, parakeets, jungle fowl, partridges, countless insects, and even the local villagers. The scientists found that the factor triggering the masting was the arrival of the El Niño Southern Oscillation, a periodic shift in tropical ocean circulation patterns that bring drought to Indonesia between June and August. Masting follows the drought. It is an amazing evolutionary strategy of an entire population of trees.

Some biologists think masting is also part of a tree's strategy to control predators. By interspersing mast years with long periods of nutlessness, trees subject animals that depend on seeds and nuts for their existence to feast-and-famine cycles. If the famine lasts long enough, the animal population crashes and the trees are safe, at least for a while. In China, some bamboo species produce seeds only once in a hundred years, and then die, causing starvation in bamboo-eating pandas.

SEED-EATING *S*QUIRRELS AND SONGBIRDS

In the Douglas-fir forest, the main seed-eating predator is the Douglas squirrel (*Tamiasciurus douglasii*), a 20-centimeter-long (8-inch-long) bluish gray bundle of energy with a bright buff belly and eye rings, black ears, and a tail shorter than its body. During the summer, the Douglas squirrel sits on the higher branches, cuts off a maturing cone, and begins systematically to strip it bare; it peels the scales off one at a time, starting at the bottom, eating the seeds at the cone's base, and dropping the empty scale and eventually the stripped axis to the ground. Now, in the fall, the squirrels frantically pluck thousands of seed cones from the trees before the seeds disperse. The squirrels cut the cones off at the stem, let them fall to the ground, then scurry down to cache them in holes under fallen logs and stumps, where they remain moistened and do not shed their seeds. A good many cones are loosely buried in the forest floor, and some of their seeds will germinate and sprout. The squirrels work with astonishing speed and efficiency. One observed in California cut off 537 redwood cones in thirty minutes; it took the squirrel four days to cache its harvest. John Muir, who greatly admired the diligence of this small mammal, estimated that up to 50 percent of the forest's cone production passes through the energetic paws of Douglas squirrels.

Like their close relatives the red squirrels (*Tamiasciurus hudsonicus*), Douglas squirrels are fiercely territorial, each individual defending a range in the mature Douglas-fir forest of about a hectare (2½ acres). With its shrill, chattering cry, it defends its home from flying squirrels, chipmunks, and especially other Douglas squirrels, including potential mates. Within this area it makes a summer nest, or drey, in the forks of the higher boughs, sometimes appropriating an abandoned hawk's or raven's nest. In the fall it abandons the nest for a winter den in a cavity in a tree's trunk, created when a large lower branch breaks off and rainwater seeps in and rots out a hollow—often aided by insects, woodpeckers, and red-shafted flickers. The squirrel lines the cavity with shredded bark and needles and fills the bottom with seeds as an emergency supply. It does not go into deep hibernation during the winter but naps for days at a time, awakens to nibble from its cache, and naps again.

In the spring it begins its own reproductive cycle, which follows that of the tree. During its courtship and mating sessions in April, it feeds on Douglas-fir and lodgepole pine pollen; when the young are born in mid-May, the parents feast on the tree's young terminal buds and shoots. The young are nursed for eight weeks, until the middle of July, after which they are ejected from the natal nest and are on their own. Now the yearlings have to forage for their winter food supply, and they switch to eating mature seed cones, thereby coming into competition with adults that have already established their territories. The difficulty first-year adults have in finding and defending their own territories is what keeps the Douglas squirrel population from taking over the Earth; many of them never find their own niche, fail to cache enough food for the winter, and die of starvation before spring, a problem that is exacerbated by the continuing depletion of the old-growth Douglas-fir forest.

During the first week of September, in time for seed burst, songbirds begin to arrive on their fall migrations. For some, like the dark-eyed juncos, this is as far south as they go; they will join the resident juncos, which have been here all summer. All juncos are now called dark-eyed, but there are two forms in these western forests: those that used to be called slate-sided and those formerly known as Oregon juncos. The slate-sided juncos have solid, ash-colored upper parts (dark gray hoods and breasts, wings, and tails), waistcoats of pale buff feathers, and two snow-white outer tail feathers that flash like sparks in the dark underbrush when they put on their air brakes for a landing. The Oregon juncos have dark hoods, but the rest of their upper bodies are reddish brown, with a darker, rust-colored patch across their shoulders and slightly rufous sides. Both types are called *Junco hyemalis,* from the Latin word for "rushes," the Juncaceae. Someone at some point must have thought that juncos fed on rush seeds, but they do not. In the spring they feed their nestlings on spiders and insect larvae, but now, in autumn, the adults eat a wide variety of plant seeds, not including rushes, foraging in the sunny meadows and at the edges of the forest. They spend most of their feeding time on the ground, where they move about in their two-footed hop known as the double-scratch: one hop forward, feet coming down on a stalk of grass seeds, and then a quick hop backward to peck at the fallen seeds.

Juncos and the forest's other overwintering birds—pine siskins, song sparrows, golden-throated sparrows, red crossbills, and purple finches—also feed copiously on Douglas-fir seeds, which at the end of September cover the ground like tiny, dry, transparent fish. Birds eat them because they are large and contain enough starch to make the effort of breaking them open worthwhile. In non-mast years, fructivorous birds account for the consumption of as much as 65 percent of the tree's annual production of seeds.

For some visiting birds, like the sparrows, migrating from the northern forest to the south, September is a temporary stopover during which they top up their carbohydrates. Some of them will gorge on Douglas-fir seeds, then continue south and excrete those seeds with their fecal matter along the Pacific coast. Others, having eaten their fill of seeds, will in their turn be eaten by American kestrels, red-tailed hawks, and rough-legged hawks, their crops ripped open and the seeds dispersed or else ingested by the hawks and deposited in the hawks' own droppings. In this way seeds from the old-growth forest in the north spread and change the forest composition in the southern latitudes. Over hundreds and thousands of years, this migration of birds and therefore trees has changed the weather and erosion patterns of the southern areas, because water transpired by a forest affects the hydrologic cycle and wind traveling over trees is different from wind blowing over naked soil.

TREES FIGHT BACK

The tree has flourished despite being an attractive target for a host of predators—birds, squirrels, and black-tailed deer, which like to graze on seeds and tender Douglas-fir shoots; fungi determined to penetrate the pithy core; insects attracted to buds and needles; and various bacteria and viruses searching for ways to enter through the cell walls. Unable to swat a pest or move out of its way, plants depend on an arsenal of chemical weapons with which to defend themselves from invading pathogens. A healthy plant is an efficient biochemical factory that continuously produces chemical compounds, some to enhance growth and others, called secondary compounds, that have more to do with defending the tree from invading enemies. Most of the medicinal and recreational uses to which humans have put plants over the centuries, from ancient herbal medicines to modern pharmaceutical drugs, are derived from these secondary products. They fall under three main categories: terpenes, phenolics, and alkaloids.

Some terpenes aid the tree's growth—the hormone gibberellic acid is terpene based, for example—but most are used for defense. Resin contains mono- and diterpenes. Resin flows up and down the tree's stem and branches and even into its needles and cones through special ducts within the grain. When an insect larva bores into a tree, it risks puncturing one of these ducts; when that happens, resin pours into the insect's feeding chamber. As if that weren't deterrent enough, resin contains terpenes that further kill the insect's appetite. The resin then hardens, sealing the wound to prevent fungal spores from getting in. A badly infested tree may have hundreds of resin plugs protruding from the bark. Some terpenes are toxic. Milkweed plants, for example, contain a terpene that is toxic to birds, which is why monarch butterfly larvae gorge on them; the ingested molecules act to diminish bird predation of the insect. The active insecticidal compound in neem oil, a medicinal extract in neem trees, is a triterpene.

Phenolics are benzene based and often volatile—they can travel great distances through the air. Some phenolics, called flavonoids, are responsible for the odors and colors by which a flower attracts pollinating insects. Other phenolics are elements in plant allelopathy, the ability of one plant to inhibit the growth of other plants in the same ecosystem: black walnut trees, for example, secrete a compound from their roots that prevents many plants from growing directly beneath their canopies. Some desert plants emit a phenolic—salicylic acid, the compound from which aspirin is derived—that stops neighboring plant roots from absorbing water.

Sometimes the influence is positive, however, as when phenolic emissions alert neighboring plants of the same species to an imminent invasion of defoliating insects. In an experiment conducted in 1979, three groups of willow trees were planted in pots and placed in sealed rooms, two groups in one room and the third group in another. Half of the trees in the first room were infected with leaf-eating caterpillars. After two weeks, the immune systems in the infected plants had been cranked up to repel the caterpillar invasion, and so were the immune systems in the uninfected trees in the same room; the trees in the isolated room, however, were unaffected. Somehow the infested trees in the first room alerted the other trees in that room—and not by mycorrhizal communication, because the trees were in pots. Some volatile compound emitted by the infected group had set off a master switch in their neighbors.

When a plant is under attack by a herbivorous insect, it can also emit phenolic compounds that attract other insects that feed on the invader. Experiments with wild tobacco, for example, have shown that when the plant's leaves are being eaten by hawkmoth caterpillars, the plant emits odoriferous compounds that attract *Geocoris pallens*, an oviparous insect that feeds on hawkmoth eggs. Apparently, a chemical contained in the caterpillars' saliva triggers the SOS emission. Similar phenomena have been observed in ginkgo trees, corn, and cotton plants. According to Marcel Dicke, a Dutch plant biologist who has studied chemical emissions from lima beans, "plants talking to their bodyguards is likely to be a characteristic of most, if not all, plant species." Plants call upon a vast array of mites and parasitic wasps to come to their aid, and predatory insects have evolved the ability to monitor the air for these chemical signals.

Tannins are polymerized flavonoids, which protect a tree's tissue from microbial decay—they perform the same function when used to "tan" leather. In oaks, chestnuts, and conifers they also work as feeding repellents by damaging a herbivore's gut; tannins disrupt the gut epithelium membrane and inhibit the animal from being able to digest what it eats. As a result, some herbivores, such as deer and bears, must often eat masses of leaves to obtain enough nourishment to maintain their weight. Animals eat for nitrogen, and plants take advantage of this need by varying the amount of nitrogen in their leaves so that herbivores, including insects, must travel from one part of a tree to another, or from one tree to another, or better yet from one species to another, to find fodder with adequate amounts of nitrogen.

Even at that, plants keep their nitrogen count as low as possible. Trees have the lowest proportion of all plants—as low as .0003 percent in xylem, up to 5 percent in leaves, and 8 percent in buds and new shoots. Most insects need to maintain between 9 and

15 percent in their bodies to reproduce. Plants also mix their nitrogen with phenolic toxins, such as tannins and alkaloids, to make their leaves and seeds unpalatable. The seasonal migration of herbivores, including deer, bison, and insects, is partly explained by their perpetual quest for nitrogen-rich grazing and may therefore be said to be under the control of plants.

Alkaloids, the third category of secondary chemical compounds produced by plants, can pass through cell membranes as easily as light through glass. They travel straight to the central nervous system, where they trigger reactions in the brain. Caffeine, for example, mimics adrenaline, which is why it gives us only the illusion of wakefulness. Coffee addicts are perpetually frustrated adrenaline junkies. Nicotine, an alkaloid of tobacco, travels to the brain ten times as fast as caffeine and is therefore that much more addictive. Morphine is the principal alkaloid of opium and is also highly addictive.

Not all alkaloids are harmful. Quinine, essential for the prevention of malaria, is an alkaloid of the bark of the cinchona tree. Atropine, isolated from roots of *Atropa belladonna*, is used as a respiratory stimulant and an antispasmodic. But most alkaloids are poisonous when ingested in sufficient quantities. Strychnine is an alkaloid of the Southeast Asian poison nut (*Strychnos nux-vomica*); a weak solution of it was used in the nineteenth century as a cure for alcoholism, but a slightly stronger dose causes extremely painful death. Nicotine was developed as a treatment for scabies and, in stronger doses, for epilepsy (or, as it was called at the time, brain-fag); effects of an overdose include loss of consciousness and possibly death. Nervocidine, derived from the East Indian gasubasu tree (a member of the Erythrophloeum or ironwood family), was used by dentists in place of arsenic as an analgesic, no doubt to many patients' relief, but it was also injected subcutaneously, at a dosage of 1 micromilligram per kilogram (2.2 pounds) of body weight, to kill dogs. The attempt to find an opium derivative less addictive than morphine backfired when it produced a compound that was actually twenty times as addictive: heroin.

Some of the plants in our forest contain deadly alkaloids. Most are members of the beautiful lily family. The death camas (*Zigadenus venenosus*), for example, has a delicate yellow flower that looks like and grows beside the true camas (*Camassia quamash*), whose roots are edible; Native peoples visiting "camas prairies" in the forest during times of food shortages would have to exercise extreme caution in distinguishing between the two plants. Western false hellebore (*Veratrum californicum*) also grows in the area, often in the understory of stands of quaking aspen; when eaten by ewes on the fourteenth day of gestation, it causes cyclops tetrogenicity—lambs born with a single eye in the middle of their foreheads. To induce sterility, Native people boiled the root to make an infusion, which was taken three times a day for three weeks. Green hellebore (*V. viride*) is highly toxic as a young plant, although after first frost an infusion of the leaves was used by Native peoples to lower blood pressure. When the plant is dried and powdered, it is sold as the garden insecticide Hellebore. Dioscorides knew white hellebore, the roots of which he said could be dried, ground, mixed with honey, and used to kill mice.

SEEDS AND SEX

Since birds consume up to 65 percent of a year's seed production and Douglas squirrels, mice, voles, and chipmunks take care of a good part of the rest, it is not surprising that fewer than one-tenth of 1 percent of Douglas-fir seeds survive where they fall to become new trees. Producing massive amounts of seed is one way trees compensate for such huge losses. Douglas-fir seed production is piffling compared with that of some flowering plants—a single capsule of some orchids, for example, can contain up to 4 million seeds and has a much lower rate of success than a Douglas-fir. Medieval philosophers such as Saint Thomas Aquinas (who had been a student and then a colleague of Albertus Magnus in Cologne and Paris), attempting to graft Aristotelian principles onto Christian doctrine—to make a synthesis of reason and faith—saw in this abundant seed production evidence of the Creator's grand design. Nature was "the Book of God's work," and seed overproduction was part of Nature's plenitude; sufficient seeds had to be produced to feed all the animals, including humans, with enough left over to perpetuate the species. Thus, overproduction was seen both as a sign of Divine Providence and as the result of a natural cause.

The biblical metaphor "All flesh is grass" can be taken literally; almost everything we eat is either a plant itself or an animal that lives on plants. Humans rarely eat carnivores. The only meat eaters in our regular diets, apart from insectivorous birds, are fish, many of which are farmed—the best known being salmon. Farming carnivores is grossly inefficient; 3 to 5 kilograms (6½ to 11 pounds) of perfectly edible fish, rendered into pellets, are required to grow each kilogram (2.2 pounds) of salmon. It's like feeding goats and sheep to lions and then eating the lions.

We now realize that the layer of arable soil is a thin hope on which to pin the fate of human culture. If the planet were reduced to the size of a basketball, soil on the surface would be the thickness of an atom. Yet we abuse this fragile layer terribly by using chemicals in agriculture and by dumping our toxic waste into it. If all flesh *is* grass, it is in our own interest to take better care of the grass.

To the early divines, seeking to reconcile theology with what they were learning about science, it made sense that Divine Order would ensure that plants produced enough seed to feed Creation and to keep Creation going. The chief proponent of this view in seventeenth-century England was John Ray, who has been called the founder of British natural history. A Catholic priest who later lectured in Greek and mathematics, Ray became interested in botany and wrote papers on the motion of sap in trees, on germination, on the number of species, and on differences between them. In the last two papers, like many botanists of his time, he was working on a system of taxonomy, searching for a consistent and reliable method for organizing the plant kingdom based on characteristics of their seeds, fruits, and roots. Some universal method was needed to impose order on the chaos of new information that seemed to be arriving daily in the fields of botany and zoology.

Ray flirted with the idea of plant sexuality, a scandalous notion in Puritan England but one that was becoming fashionable in Europe. A generation earlier, the English botanist Nehemiah Grew had proposed that a plant's anthers were its male sex organs, and Ray tended to agree with him—perhaps, being no Puritan, even wondering about its female parts. Uniting plants and animals in such a way might make it easier to find a universal system of classification. But it would be nearly half a century before anyone publicly expressed such thoughts, and then it would be an Italian—Camerarius—followed by a Frenchman, Sébastien Vaillant.

Vaillant was in charge of the collection at Paris's Jardin du Roi (later Jardin des Plantes). He oversaw the construction of France's first greenhouse in 1714 and eventually became a professor at the Jardin; his opening lecture—on the existence of sexuality in plants, an extension of the views of La Brosse and the first public expression of Camerarius's ideas in France—was delivered in September 1717 and was so popular that although Vaillant delivered it at six o'clock in the morning he filled the auditorium. The tree that he used for his demonstrations, a pistachio, is still growing in the Alpine garden of the Muséum d'histoire naturelle. After Vaillant's death in 1722, the lecture was published and continued to create a stir. Perhaps its most far-reaching effect was that it was avidly read by a young, impoverished Swedish student at the University of Uppsala named Carl von Linné, later and better known as Carolus Linnaeus.

Although the notion that plants had sexual identities was not new, what Vaillant contributed, and what sparked Linnaeus's interest, was the idea that a plant's sex organs were so consistent within various species that they could be used as the basis for a system of classification. Other systems of the time depended on such vague and subjective determinations as the shape of a plant's flower or its color or size. What Linnaeus proposed was the straightforward, mathematical counting—what Stephen Jay Gould has called "the dry anatomy of numbers"—of its reproductive organs.

At the time, the field of taxonomy was as complex as a Byzantine emperor's bloodline—more than three hundred systems for organizing the natural world were in use. Linnaeus's fundamentals, established after reading Vaillant's paper, were crushingly simple. Theophrastus had already identified specimens according to genus and species; Linnaeus simply added two more categories above them—class and order—and devised an easy way of placing each organism into its appropriate slot. A plant's class is determined by the number and arrangement of its stamens (male organs, a filament bearing an anther); its order is determined by the number and arrangement of its carpels (female organs). His system was to plants what the Dewey decimal system is to books: there were twenty-four classes, dozens of orders, hundreds of genera, and thousands of species. The whole world was like a great library, in which each species had its own place on the right shelf (genus) in the proper section (order) of the correct floor (class)—and not just every known species but, equally important, every new species that came into the library. The class and order of every plant could be determined in the field as easily as in the laboratory by anyone with a magnifying glass and the ability to count to twenty. (A plant with one stamen was in the class Monandria—"one man"; if two, it was Diandria, and so on up to twenty, Icosandria. The class for plants with more than twenty stamens was simply called Polyandria.) After Linnaeus, the business of classifying new plants was practically routine.

The taxonomic system developed by Linnaeus is still the main classificatory form in use today, although a few new categories have been added. All life on Earth has been divided into three huge domains: Bacteria, Archaea, and Eukarya. Humans are descended from the eukaryotes, which broke off from bacteria perhaps 2 billion years ago. A human being is thus taxonomically defined as follows: Domain: Eukarya; Kingdom: Animalia; Phylum: Chordata; Class: Mammalia; Order: Primates; Family: Hominidae; Genus: *Homo;* Species: *sapiens.* The Douglas-fir's taxonomic ID is:

Domain: Eukarya; Kingdom: Plantae; Phylum: Coniferophyta; Class: Pinopsida; Order: Pinales; Family: Pinaceae; Genus: *Pseudotsuga;* Species: *menziesii.*

None of which, it seems to some, really defines an organism. In fact, the simplicity of Linnaeus's classification became the chief objection to it. It was almost as though Linnaeus had taken the fun out of botany (as Melvil Dewey may be said to have taken the pleasure out of book browsing). Never mind the plump beauty of the fruit, the graceful arc of its stalk as it bends over a mountain brook, or the dazzling effect of a mass of flowers arranged against a shimmering meadow after rain; how many stamens does it have? How many carpels? Linnaeus himself tried to soften the cold anatomy of numbers in his own writing. In 1729 he described a plant with a single stamen and a single pistil as though it were a bride and groom on their wedding night: "The flower's leaves . . . serve as a bridal bed which the Creator has so gloriously arranged, adorned with such noble bed curtains, and perfumed with so many soft scents that the bridegroom with his bride might there celebrate their nuptials in greater solemnity." But it was no use. Linnaeus's is a dry system, with the serendipity leached out of it, perhaps necessarily so. "The ingenuity and utility of this system are indisputable," Darwin wrote in his sole reference to Linnaeus in *The Origin of Species.* The Swedish naturalist thought his system revealed the inner workings of God's mind. "But unless it be specified whether order in time or space, or both, or what else is meant by the plan of the Creator," Darwin wrote, "it seems to me that nothing is thus added to our knowledge."

Writer John Fowles, visiting Linnaeus's own garden, now a carefully preserved shrine behind Linnaeus's former house in

Uppsala, echoed Darwin's caveat. Fowles was conscious that he was standing at ground zero of an explosion "whose radiations and mutations inside the human brain were incalculable and continue to be so"—Linnaeus's tiny plot of soil is "the place where an intellectual seed landed and is now grown to a tree that shadows the entire globe." But Fowles is, he confesses, "a heretic about Linnaeus." He rebels against the individuation of plants that Linnaeus sought so hard to make possible, the reduction of natural phenomena to a specific class within a certain order. He sees it as the first step toward anthropocentrism, in which we define Nature only in terms of our place in it or outside of it. Linnaeus's system, he says, requires us to abandon "certain possibilities of seeing, apprehending and experiencing" in exchange for categorizing and labeling; it is like viewing Nature through the viewfinder of a camera. "And that," he writes, "is the bitter fruit from the tree of Uppsalan knowledge."

In recent times, the ability to extract and compare DNA has provided a new appreciation for the accuracy, if not the beauty, of Linnaeus's insight. Although more complicated than counting carpels and stamens, DNA analysis is a powerful tool with which to determine the degree of relatedness between seemingly unrelated species. The key to DNA's power is the arrangement of four molecular structures, known as bases, which are identified simply by their first letters: A for adenine, T for thymine, G for guanine, and C for cytosine. The four bases are strung along a molecular string in a linear array, and two strings of DNA spiral about each other with the bases arranged in pairs: A on one string always pairs with T on the other string, and G always pairs with C. The sequence of bases along one string forms a message, or a sentence, spelled out in successive three-letter words. (Geneticists speak of a species' total DNA package as its "book.")

The tendency of the bases to form pairs is a useful property. If a solution of DNA molecules is heated until the bonding between the bases is broken, the paired strands separate and float freely. Upon cooling slowly, the bases apparently collide and begin to reform in pairs. The pairing of sequences is so specific that double-stranded molecules are reconstituted. If DNA from one species is mixed with DNA from a different species, and the solution is heated and then slowly cooled, a strand of DNA from one species may find a sequence of the other species' DNA that is similar to its own, and the two strands may zip together to form a hybrid species. Such hybrids can be measured, and the proportion of each species that forms such hybrids can be determined. If a high proportion of each species' DNA forms hybrids with the other's, we know that the two original species were closely related, since they must have had a large number of similar sequences. In a great many instances, affinities between species as determined by DNA analysis coincide closely with relationships observed or predicted by Linnaeus.

Wings and Wind

Each species in its niche solves its own problems or dies, and the ingenuity of the solutions is as varied as the number of species and niches. And having overcome one obstacle, a species does not necessarily resort to the same solution when a similar problem crops up. It might seem that a sensible plant, having dealt satisfactorily with the problem of pollen dispersal, for example, would simply apply the same strategy to dispersing its seeds. But that almost never happens.

Tree

Pollen and seed dispersal have very different goals. A tree may find it advantageous to distribute its pollen as far and widely as possible so that a given individual's chances of spreading its genetic material is maximized. But it isn't necessarily a good idea to let one's apples fall too far from the parent tree. Having pollinated a distant tree, the pollinator should probably allow that tree to take care of its seeds while it looks after its own. Although becoming established in a mycorrhizal mat is difficult for a seedling, being close to the parent can be beneficial to the offspring, since their roots will grow down into the same mycorrhizal mat as the parent's. Not only are the young assured of finding appropriate fungi, but by tapping into an existing underground network of shared nutrients they also extend it, thereby aiding both offspring and parent. Although it may seem that in a myccorhizal community the larger trees have the greater drawing power and prosper at the expense of the smaller, in fact, proportionally, larger trees contribute more stored carbohydrates to the system than smaller trees do. A parent tree actually feeds its young, just as a bear or yellow warbler would. Also, plants that do not self-pollinate obviously do better when surrounded closely by plants of the same species.

Although Douglas-fir relies on the wind to disperse both its pollen and its seeds, it makes certain that its pollen is blown as far as possible and that its seeds stay relatively close at hand. Douglas-fir seeds have a single wing attached to catch the autumn breezes, a common but not universal feature in conifers, but because they are heavy they rarely fly far from home. Some other conifers don't want their children to roam at all. Lodgepole pines (*Pinus contorta*), for example, retain their seed cones, with the seeds inside them, for up to seventy-five years; if there is no fire to release them, the cones drop from the tree with the seeds still inside, and only when the cones decompose are the seeds released. The knobcone pine (*P. attenuata*) is even more possessive; it holds onto its seeds so long that its bark actually grows over its seed cones and the seeds are not released until the parent tree dies, crashes to the ground, and, in rotting, serves as compost for its own offspring.

Other winged seeds and fruits travel farther. Elms and ashes supply their fruits with two wings. As a result, they twirl to the ground more slowly and therefore travel farther afield than a nut would. In the coniferous forests of eastern North America, the pitch pine (*Pinus rigida*) does not release all its winged seeds at once in the fall but staggers their release throughout the winter; the seeds fall on snow and ice and continue to be transported by wind and by spring runoff. Thoreau observed that a pitch-pine seed "thus crossed one of our ponds, which is half a mile wide, and I see no reason why it should not be blown many miles in some cases," along a frozen river, for instance, or across a series of meadows. The biggest winged seed is that of the Brazilian arariba, or zebrawood, tree (*Centrolobium robustum*); its wingspan is 17 centimeters (6½ inches), and its seed spirals gracefully to the ground at a gentle angle, like a glider when it runs out of wind.

Not all wind-dispersed seeds are winged. Some have parachutes—dandelion seeds, for example, or those of the South African silver tree. Some, like the bladder senna, have balloons; their seed pods inflate and, when detached from the plant, float great distances in the air. The stamens of the small Antarctic plant known as feathery mistletoe, after delivering their pollen to the ovule, rearrange themselves into long plumes that remain attached to the seed and act as sails. We don't think of tumbleweed as a seed-dispersal unit, but that's what it is. When the seeds are dry and ready to germinate, the spiny saltwort detaches itself from its root, curls up into a ball, and lets the wind bounce it across the plains, scattering seeds every time it hits the ground. Gourds seem to have been designed for water transport, but some desert-dwelling gourd seed cases are dispersed by wind. They dry up, become as light as air, and roll across the sand until they lodge in a wet patch, hopefully at an oasis, whereupon the sun warms them and they burst open, scattering their tiny black seeds to the wind.

Water dispersal is almost as popular, especially in the southern latitudes, where most of the Earth's surface is water, and in the tropics, where the water is warm and still and nourishing. Waterborne seeds must be buoyant and waterproof. Some, like those of the flag iris, contain air pockets that keep them afloat. Some seeds are coated in cork, others in wax, still others in oil. Coconuts are veritable coracles and can remain afloat for years. Seeds that fall into the oceans must also be able to tolerate salt.

Darwin, who maintained several acres of gardens behind his house at Down, Kent, was very interested in the question of seed dispersal and conducted exhaustive experiments to understand how it worked. In his greenhouse he had tanks filled with salt water in which he kept all manner of bizarre combinations: naked seeds, seeds in pods, seeds in the crops of dead birds, green seeds, ripe seeds, seeds attached to branches, and seeds encased in soil. He was attempting to prove that seeds could float from a mainland to offshore islands, or from one island to another, and yet remain viable. Most botanists doubted that they could and proposed ingenious methods of transportation to explain how plants native to

Europe, for example, were found growing in the Azores. Land bridges were the most common explanation; some seriously proposed that the now-lost continent of Atlantis was the answer. Darwin decided to find out if "we are not authorized in admitting such enormous geographical changes within the period of existing species." He thought we were not.

He reported the results of his experiments in *The Origin of Species*. "To my surprise," he wrote, "I found that out of eighty-seven kinds, sixty-four germinated after an emersion [in the salt-water tank] of twenty-eight days, and a few survived an emersion of a hundred and thirty-seven days." Dried hazelnuts remained viable for ninety days; a dried asparagus plant floated for eighty-five days, whereupon its seeds germinated in the usual manner. He concluded that 14 percent of the seeds of any country "might be floated by sea-currents during twenty-eight days, and would retain their power of germination." That would, he calculated, allow them to travel up to 1,500 kilometers (about 900 miles) by sea and still grow into plants when they arrived. When added to the number of seeds transported in the crops of birds and deposited in their guano, seeds trapped in the soil attached to floating tree trunks, and seeds fed upon by marine animals—those of the Galápagos tomato, for example, will only germinate after having spent two to three weeks in the gut of a giant tortoise—the ability of plants to spread themselves over great distances, even across wide oceans, was not something that required a lost continent to explain.

Darwin was interested in seed overproduction and dispersal because they conformed to his hypothesis of evolution by natural selection. They explained one way in which new species were born. Plants produce more seeds than they need because only a percentage of them are viable in their place of origin. Even in an average year, as many as 60 percent of a Douglas-fir's seeds will be unsound; in poor seed years, the percentage rises to 82. Many of the rest will land in unfavorable spots, be destroyed by fire, or be eaten by insects, birds, or animals. Some of the surviving seeds, however, will have slight variations at the genetic level that make them unsuited to their native habitat but might be more viable in a distant environment or an environment with a different climate. Seeds bearing these new genetic combinations, when transported to a distant location by wind, birds, animals, icebergs, glacial movement, or some other means, may find themselves in a habitat that favors their particular hereditary makeup. They would, at first, be the same species as the parent, but in time, as they adapted to their new environment, they would become an allied species, clearly revealing their relatedness to the parental species by their affinities (similarly sequenced strands of DNA, for example) but through isolation diverging to eventually become a distinct species that could no longer interbreed with the originating species to produce a fertile hybrid.

THE OLD-GROWTH COMMUNITY

Our tree is more than 250 years old and is now part of an old-growth forest. An old-growth Douglas-fir forest differs from a younger forest in many ways. It is composed of even-aged trees and snags—standing dead trunks, without bark or branches, often hollow in the center. Although the forest is dominated by centuries-old Douglas-firs, there is an understory of other species waiting to take over, which makes the forest floor perpetually shaded and damp. In the rare open spaces left by fallen giants, a layer of lower broadleaf trees and shrubs—vine maples, salmon-berries, and red huckleberries—takes advantage of the unaccustomed light. Among the ferns covering the forest floor is a litter of fallen branches and huge trunks in various stages of decay. Flying squirrels live in the snags and fill their hollows with droppings. The bird regime also changes. Whereas a forest that is from 50 to 100 years old supports low-branch-nesting species such as Swainson's thrushes, Townsend's warblers, and Wilson's warblers, a 250-year-old stand is home to western flycatchers, brown creepers, boreal chickadees, and varied thrushes, birds that nest in cavities or under loose bark. These birds are all insectivorous and so play a vital role in determining which insect species thrive and which are kept in check.

In the area where our tree is, 140 species of defoliating insects specialize in conifer trees in general; 51 of them are specific to Douglas-fir. These include the Douglas-fir beetle, the Douglas-fir tussock moth, the balsam fir sawfly, the brownlined looper, the greenstriped forest looper, the phantom hemlock looper, and the western blackheaded budworm. The western spruce budworm is not yet a pest here—the first outbreak will not be recorded until 1909. In all trees, defoliating insects eat needles as well as the young buds that would otherwise form needles, shoots, and cones. In Douglas-fir, the phantom hemlock looper (*Nepytia phantasmaria*) lays its eggs on the underside of some needles in October. When the larvae emerge in late May, they immediately begin to gorge on the needles and continue to do so until they pupate in mid-August. The adults emerge in September, mate, and lay eggs, and the cycle is repeated. An unchecked phantom hemlock looper infestation can kill a tree the size of a mature Douglas-fir in a matter of years.

Fortunately for the tree, the larvae of these insects are devoured by a number of bird species, including pine grosbeaks, various warblers, thrushes and sparrows, western flycatchers, western tanagers, pine siskins, and cedar waxwings.

The trees get help from other outside sources as well, some of them unlikely. Carpenter ants, for instance, are generally thought to be destructive to trees, but they do most of their damage to wood that has already fallen and started to decay. Certain species actually aid trees by feeding on the eggs, larvae, and pupae of defoliating insects. This makes a certain amount of sense, since ants depend on healthy trees for much of the year. Although carpenter ants form vast colonies in the soft wood of decaying trunks lying on the forest floor, they spend a lot of their time foraging in the canopy. Apart from eating insects, they also tend their aphid farms. Much of a carpenter ant's diet consists of "honeydew"—excess sugars and fecal matter secreted from the anus of aphids. The ants gather aphid eggs in the fall and store them in their colonies during the winter. In the spring they place the eggs out on plants, allow them to hatch, then tend and milk the aphids throughout the summer. They even defend their aphid herds from attacks by predators. A Central and South American species of carpenter ant, *Camponotus femoratus,* has developed the ant-plant symbiosis even further; it builds "ant gardens" in the rain forest canopy. These are tight, hollow balls of chewed vegetable matter filled with soil and wedged into the forks of branches. Inside these nests, the ants place the seeds of plants they prefer to eat—bromeliads, figs, pipers—and the plants sprout and grow within the gardens. Some of these tended plants are found nowhere else but in ant gardens, meaning that the ants must gather all the seeds from those plants and resow them year after year.

The species of carpenter ants in the Douglas-fir forest, *Camponotus modoc*, is the hub of a vast and intricate ecological web that links plants, other insects, birds, and mammals. They are the forest's chief soil makers, taking the place of earthworms by transporting huge amounts of soil to the surface, reducing wood fiber and fallen needles to humus, then mixing it with mineral soils, aerating it, and improving drainage. They participate in the seed dispersal of many plants. They eat sawfly and tussock moth larvae—a study conducted in 1990 estimated that ants accounted for an 85 percent reduction in sawfly pupae in forests in Washington and Oregon. Virtually every rotting piece of wood on the forest floor has its carpenter ant colony, some of them containing up to ten thousand workers; carpenter ants thus form a significant proportion of the forest's total biomass. It is no wonder that Harvard's ant specialist, E.O. Wilson, suggests that although human extinction would result in the disappearance of only a handful of species dependent on our armpits, groin, or insides, and the rest of nature would rebound in abundance, the disappearance of all ants would lead to total ecological collapse. Ants are the chief food of northern flickers and from mid-June to late July are even the main source of nutrition for grizzly bears.

Since bears are omnivorous, eating everything from skunk cabbage and nettles to mountain sheep, they can occupy a wide range of habitats and once roamed the length and breadth of North America. A single grizzly requires a vast area for its home range, but humans are increasingly encroaching on bear habitat. Today most grizzly populations are found in the mountains, but they were originally also numerous on the plains, feeding on bison all the way to the east coast of North America and south into Texas and Mexico. Grizzly skulls have been found in Quebec and northern Labrador.

The ancestors of the grizzlies certainly did cross the ancient Beringian land bridge, following migrant reindeer and bison herds, before the peak of the last glacial period; grizzly bear bones found in a cave on Prince of Wales Island, off the coast of Alaska, have been dated as 35,000 years old. All along the Pacific shore, coastal peoples as well as Europeans have either explained or frightened themselves with stories about bears: white bears, black bears, blue bears, brown bears, grizzled bears. Bears so big that when they scrambled up a mountain they dislodged enough earth to cause rivers to change their course. Bears that turned into people, bears that became islands. Bears that came from the north walking on their hind feet, leaving tracks that looked uncannily human. Human tracks with claws as long as the toes. In 1811, David Thompson, canoeing down the Athabasca River, saw bear tracks and thought they must have been mammoth tracks, "mammoth" being his translation of the creature his Native guides called Sasquatch, the wild man of the mountains.

As Douglas-fir seeds settle gently on the forest floor, the female grizzly that has been pulverizing rotting wood near the base of our tree for the past three days in search of carpenter ants suddenly heads uphill to the mountain meadows to feast on blueberries. Few large animals have ever dwelled permanently in the old-growth forest; its littered floor makes it difficult to get around, and its darkness and dampness make for poor foraging for herbivores. Black-tailed deer and wapiti prefer the higher meadows, and therefore so do grizzlies. During the summer months, however, the big bears feed mostly on vegetation and venture into the cool forest for ferns and the woolly cow parsnips that grow along the stream edges. But since they lack the digestive tracts of ruminants such as deer and

Grizzly bear at salmon stream

wapiti, and so do not double-digest their food, they have to eat as much as 45 kilograms (100 pounds) of vegetable matter a day to stay healthy. For a small female, that could be almost a third of her body weight. This is why she turns to ants and, when the occasion arises, mice, voles, and Douglas squirrels, for supplemental protein.

When the salmon begin to return to their natal rivers, which they do from late August to November, she will become a fisher. Fish belonging to the salmonid family—the nine species in the Pacific Northwest are sockeye, chinook, coho, pink, and chum salmon, as well as cutthroat, golden, Apache, and steelhead trout—are anadromous, which means they spend their adult lives in the ocean and each year return to freshwater streams to spawn.

There are 9,600 individual races or stocks of salmonids along the coast north of 40 degrees latitude, and hundreds of millions of members of each species battle their way up the thirteen hundred rivers and streams that empty into the Pacific Ocean. When the salmon return to their natal waters, the entire forest community feasts. From the seals and killer whales that gorge on them in bays and estuaries to the birds and mammals that form a feeding gauntlet all the way up to their spawning gravels, salmon and their eggs and offspring feed a myriad other creatures, including human beings.

The pink salmon that spawn in the stream that runs by our tree are especially adapted to old-growth forests, where the dense forest canopy shades them from direct sunlight and keeps the water temperature low. Decaying vegetation supports populations of bacteria, fungi, and invertebrates that will feed salmon fry when they hatch. Fallen logs and branches in the water not only form minor obstructions to the flow, which helps to aerate the stream, but also create soft pebble deposits for spawning. The roots of the forest trees cling to the soil, holding back erosion that could clog the beds of clean gravel. Salmon need the forest, and when the trees are clear-cut the salmon populations plummet.

In the coastal Douglas-fir forest, a temperate rain forest with mineral-rich but nitrogen-poor soil, the lack of nitrogen is a constant limiting factor for plant growth. And yet the trees in it, like those in a tropical rain forest, grow to great heights and achieve huge girths. Nitrogen comes from a number of sources, mostly from the air after having been fixed in the soil by bacteria and plants or from lichen growing on trees. But the Douglas-fir forest also gets an important part of its nitrogen fix from the sea.

Nitrogen from land has the isotopic signature ^{14}N. In the ocean, ^{15}N, the heavier form of nitrogen, is much more common. Ecologist Tom Reimchen, of the University of Victoria in British Columbia, has been following the fate of salmon and the marine isotope of nitrogen as both travel from sea to forest. Five species of salmon—chinook, coho, sockeye, chum, and pink—leave the rivers where they were born and spend two to five years in the ocean, feeding and growing and all the while accumulating ^{15}N in their body tissues. Upon returning to freshwater to spawn, they are consumed by ravens, bald eagles, bears, wolves, and other animals, such as insects and amphibians, all of which subsequently defecate nitrogen-rich fertilizer throughout the forest. Bears do most of their feeding at night and, being solitary animals, take the fish up to 200 meters (650 feet) from the river's edge to consume them alone. The bears prefer to eat the best parts, the brains and bellies, then return to the river for another fish. In one season, a bear will spread six hundred to seven hundred salmon carcasses throughout the forest, defecating and urinating along the way. Birds and other animals spread the ^{15}N even farther away. Reimchen finds the plants along the banks of streams and rivers are rich in ^{15}N and has demonstrated a correlation between the amount of ^{15}N in a tree's annual growth rings and the size of that year's salmon run. Along stream banks and river valleys, salmon supply the largest impulse of nitrogen the forest gets each year.

Beetles and slugs consume the carcasses left by the bears, and tachinid, sarcophagid, and blowflies lay their eggs in the salmon's decaying flesh. Within days, the meat remaining on each carcass is covered with a writhing mass of maggots. Once fully grown, the larvae drop onto the forest floor, where they burrow in and overwinter as pupae. In the spring, flies emerge by the billions just in time for the northern bird migration. The birds load up on ^{15}N-laden flies. Dung beetles bury bear and wolf scat in the forest duff. As well, many salmon, after spawning, die and sink to the river bottoms, where they are soon covered with a lush coat of fungi and bacteria, which in turn is consumed by water insects, copepods, and other invertebrates. When the young salmon emerge from the gravel, the water is filled with edible organisms rich in ^{15}N from their parents. Reimchen's work eloquently demonstrates that forest and fish need each other, that they connect the air, the oceans, and even the hemispheres in a single, interdependent system.

RESIDENTS OF THE CANOPY

High above the salmon run, in the dense canopy, ants and a host of other organisms occupy what can be described as an upper Earth, a kind of cloud-cuckoo-land hovering 60 meters (200 feet) above the forest floor. About one-third of a Douglas-fir's needles—perhaps 20 million of them—fall off each year, many to the ground, but many also land and remain on the tree's wide upper branches. Over the years, this needle litter builds up into mats of significant size—up to 30 centimeters (12 inches) thick and covering collectively hundreds of square meters—and is colonized by many of the same organisms that, on the forest floor, busily turn vegetative matter into soil. Unlike the forest floor, however, the canopy litter is exposed to sunlight and rain. Eventually, the mat of decaying needles in the canopy becomes nutrient-rich soil that harbors an entire community of plants, vertebrates, fungi, and insects, entirely independent of the ground—it becomes its own unique and, until recently, unsuspected ecosystem.

At the center of this brave new world is the phylum Arthropoda. Soil-based Arthropoda include everything most people call bugs: spiders, mites, millipedes, and insects. Insects have three pairs of legs and evolved from multiply segmented creatures that had one pair of legs per segment. Over the millennia, the front pairs of legs adapted to form jaws and antennae. (In the fruit fly *Drosophila melanogaster,* mutations reveal the species' ancestral origins by converting antennae back into legs that protrude from the fly's head.) There are millions of arthropod species, and recent studies have shown that up to six thousand of them, at least three hundred new to science, can be found in the canopy layer of the Douglas-fir forest, making it a reservoir of species biodiversity unmatched anywhere outside the Amazonian rain forest. Some species, such as the tiny beetle mite *Dendroʒetes,* are unknown anywhere else in North or South America—the only other place *Dendroʒetes* has been found is Japan. Other species are found nowhere else on Earth. Each tree supports its own insect community, a rich diversity of wildlife that includes all the so-called guilds: predators, prey, parasites, scavengers, and even "tourists"—individuals such as ants that live on the ground and are just passing through. In some cases, as in tropical rain forests, entire species are confined to a single mat on a single tree. Each time a tree falls, it could be taking dozens of unique arthropod species down with it.

Soil is the terrestrial ocean. Both soil and ocean are the cradles of photosynthetic life, and both are dominated by arthropods. In the ocean, the arthropods are the crustaceans—crabs, shrimps, lobsters, and various water fleas, lice, and sand hoppers. In the soil, the arthropod niche is filled by spiders, mites, beetles, and springtails. In the canopy mats, spiders are the main predators. Some are only 20 millimeters (barely three-quarters of an inch) long and build complex webs of spun protein in which they trap flies, moths, and the seventy-two species of oribatid mites that also inhabit the mats. Mites are tiny creatures whose main function within the forest community is to break vegetable matter down into humus. Also present in the soil, although in slightly smaller populations, are the springtails, members of the Collembola family. Mites and springtails dig and delve their way through all types of soil. In open-ground meadows, 2 cubic centimeters (0.1 cubic inch) of soil generally harbors as many as fifty mites and springtails; in the forest, with its deep leaf litter, which holds moisture and also has plenty of open spaces, there may be twice that number. Up in the canopy mats, which more closely resemble open fields, their density is closer to that in meadows.

Mites, having four pairs of legs, belong to the arachnid, or spider, family, whereas springtails, with only six legs and one pair of

Wolf shelter

antennae, are more like insects than spiders. They were first described in 1873 by Darwin's neighbor and sometime collaborator, Sir John Lubbock, who was amazed by their principal means of locomotion, "a sub-abdominal forked organ that, commencing near the posterior end of the body, reaches forward in most cases as far as the thorax." When alarmed, the springtail releases this powerfully muscled organ and springs into the air, sometimes as high as 15 centimeters (6 inches), the equivalent of a human jumping the length of six football fields in a single bound. Lubbock classified mites as insects, but only because of their six legs; he added that future entomologists would no doubt conclude they were something else. American naturalist Howard Ensign Evans agrees that, with their springboard form of locomotion, "they appear to represent a separate and independent experiment in six-leggedness." Their abdomens are segmented into six sections rather than eleven, as in true insects, and they lack certain internal body parts associated with the Insecta. Salamanders do not care what they are, however; they eat them anyway, at least on the ground. In the canopy springtails, along with mites and spiders, are caught in the orb webs of larger spiders or are snapped up by red-breasted nuthatches.

Bird droppings, rodent scat, sloughed snake skins, insect frass, fresh plant matter, worked humus, rain, and sunlight make for a rich, fertile soil. So rich and fertile, in fact, that Douglas-fir trees spontaneously sprout adventitious roots from their branches to take nourishment from it. During the Carboniferous period, when rhizomous ferns were changing themselves into trees, roots started out as buds that grew on branches lying along the ground—their shoots shot into the ground rather than into the air. In the forest canopy mats, apical meristems buried under mats develop into roots instead of branches. These roots perform exactly as their subterranean counterparts do, absorbing water and minerals from the aerial soil and helping to stabilize the mats by acting as supporting struts. Perhaps not coincidentally, these new roots, buried in soil high above the ground, come into play at just about the time that the ground soil is running out of the nitrogen that was fixed in it hundreds of years ago by bacteria in the long-gone red alders.

This time the nitrogen comes from lichen. In an old-growth forest, if the upper side of a Douglas-fir branch is exposed to air, it is covered by a dense coating of yellowish-green lichen. (The underside, which receives less sunlight, is usually given to mosses and liverworts.) The relationship between lichens and trees in the forest canopy can be seen as an aerial version of the mycorrhizal fungal networks that exist below the ground; both regimes perform much the same function and are made up of much the same materials.

Lichen is not a plant in the ordinary sense; it is a composite of two plant-related organisms, fungi and algae. Lichen is a fungus wrapped around an alga, both functioning together as a single entity. It is thus a kind of living fossil plant, a direct link with the original oceanic photosynthesizers that began life in the primordial seas, filled Earth's atmosphere with oxygen, then crept onto the land and became vascular plants. Lichen is the other route the algae took to adapt to life on land; about thirty-seven genera of them formed symbiotic relationships with some thirteen orders of Ascomycetes, or "sac" fungi. Fungi have roots, which take up water, and algae photosynthesize, providing food for both parts of the organism. Each bonds with the other to become one organism, sharing both function and product. This symbiosis has been so successful that there are now nearly fourteen thousand species of lichens worldwide, existing in habitats as diverse as Antarctica and the tropics, in climates as different as coastal rain forests and alpine meadows, and on every substrate from boulders to wooden buildings to the backs of insects.

Lichens are fascinating lessons in symbiosis. To form a lichen, a fungus species encases the alga with its hyphae, pressing the hyphal tips tightly against the algal cell walls and penetrating the cells with tiny fingers, or haustoria. The alga produces sugars by photosynthesis, and the fungus takes some of those sugars—usually leaving behind enough to keep the algal cells alive—and also pumps water into the cell. The fungus shades the alga, protecting it from too much sunlight, and provides it with an enhanced photosynthesizing surface area. So far, all is symbiotic. In some cases, however, the fungus takes too great a portion of sugar, and the algal cells die—the lichen survives only because the alga reproduces cells faster than the fungus kills them. This is not, strictly speaking, a mutualistic relationship but one more accurately characterized as "controlled parasitism."

The lichen associated with the Douglas-fir canopy is *Lobaria oregana*, or lettuce lichen, a species of lungwort—there is lungwort on the top of the branch and liverwort underneath. Lungworts are so called because their tissue resembles the interior of a lung and because they are often used as remedies for such respiratory diseases as tuberculosis and asthma; a seventeenth-century translation of Pliny's *Historia Naturalis* notes that lichen "hath a wonderfull operation to cure the rhagadies or chap." A single hectare (a quarter of an acre) of old-growth Douglas-fir forest can support up to a tonne of *Lobaria,* which holds both green algae and cyanobacteria within its fungal grip. The lichen attaches itself to the tree's bark by means of tiny holdfasts and intercepts rainwater as it runs along the branches and down the trunk, extracts nitrogen from it, then releases the water to continue flowing down to the ground. When the lichen dies, it falls off the tree and accumulates either on the canopy mats or on the ground, in either case releasing its accumulated nitrogen into the soil. Lichens replace red alders as efficient nitrogen fixers; every year they provide up to 4 kilograms (9 pounds) of nitrogen to every hectare (quarter acre) of forest—80 percent of its nitrogen diet. They, too, are a vital link in the living chain of organisms that make up the Douglas-fir forest community.

OUR TREE now stands 80 meters (260 feet) high. Its first branches start at about the 40-meter (130-foot) level; they are 40 centimeters (16 inches) thick at their base and spread a wide, conical canopy over the mature forest. It has been an old-growth forest for nearly three hundred years. It has endured drought and floods, has suffered massive insect infestations, and has been shaken by storms. The winters have become colder. Its canopy mats support tonnes of wet snow, more, it seems, every year, creating enormous pressures on its limbs. Its roots remain cold and wet far into the spring. One or two branches have been broken off, and the large holes in the tree's stem have begun to soften, making pathways for fungal and insect invaders. As we have seen, a tree cannot physically repel such invasions; it can only block off the infected area, reroute its nutrients, and seal the entrance. Once an invasion has occurred, it can be contained for a while, but it cannot be reversed. Our tree now carries the seeds of its own death.

D E A T H

This solitary tree!—a living thing
Produced too slowly ever to decay;
Of form and aspect too magnificent
To be destroyed.

WORDSWORTH, "Yew Trees," 1803

Trees are by far the oldest living organisms on the planet. Some conifers, such as the coastal redwoods and giant sequoias that grow farther south, live up to three thousand years—John Muir claimed to have counted four thousand rings on a giant sequoia stump in 1880. The oldest tree in North America, a bristlecone pine known as Methuselah, now in Inyo National Park, California, may be forty-six hundred years old; in 1958, a biologist from the University of Arizona found seventeen trees older than four thousand years growing in the same park. A cypress in Chapultepec, Mexico, is believed to be more than six thousand years old. A *Cryptomeria japonica* growing on Japan's Yakusima Island has been carbon-dated to seventy-two hundred years. Tropical trees that do not produce rings are more difficult to age, but there are dragon trees on the Canary Islands thought to be more than ten thousand years old, and some cycads in Australia—fellow gymnosperms—are considered to be fourteen thousand years old and counting, although some experts claim this to be an exaggeration.

Given such longevity, it seems a shame that our tree is already, at a mere 550 years, showing signs of age. But it has lived a much less sheltered life than its longer-lived colleagues, in a cool, wet climate that requires huge expenditures of energy. Every year it has had to produce more and more new growth as its trunk has increased in girth and its crown and branches in height and length. In botany this phenomenon is known as the Red Queen syndrome; a tree always has to run faster to remain in the same place. Each year water is drawn to ever-more-distant shoots. Each spring it offers more new growth to invading insects, and each winter there are more wounded patches to heal before they become entry points for birds, ants, and wood-decaying fungi. If left alone, our tree would grow forever, but nothing in the forest is left alone.

In addition to invading insects, a Douglas-fir is known to be susceptible to thirty-one types of assaults from other plants. Most are fungal diseases, with names such as brown stringy trunk rot or Douglas-fir needle blight. These are not diseases to be taken lightly. Like mycorrhizal fungi, pathogenic fungi often specialize in a single host species and, in extreme circumstances, can wipe out virtually every individual of that species on the planet. The American elm, the former symbol of the North American urban land-scape, succumbed to a beetle-borne fungal invasion. The American sweet chestnut (*Castanea dentata*), once the most sought-after and luxurious tree in the eastern deciduous forest, is another signal example. From Maine to Alabama it grew to diameters of 4 meters (13 feet) and to heights of 40 meters (130 feet). Its edible fruit, encased in brown, *Sputnik*-like burrs, dropped in the fall and was collected in the winter. "I love to gather them," Thoreau wrote in his diary in December 1852, "if only for the sense of the bountifulness of Nature they give me." When roasted, they were a regular staple of the easterners' winter diet: "All New York goes a-nutting," Thoreau added. "Chestnuts for cabmen and newsboys, for not only are squirrels alone to be fed." Toward the end of the century, however, seedlings of a domesticated chestnut were imported from Asia; they harbored the fungus *Cryphonectria parasitica*, which causes stem rot. This fungus had a devastating impact on the native chestnuts; within fifty years, hardly a single American chestnut remained standing.

On the West Coast, root rot is brought to the forest by a number of fungi; laminated root rot, for example, is caused by *Phellinus weirii* and is especially hard on Douglas-firs, although it also infests grand fir, Pacific silver fir, subalpine fir, and mountain hemlock. The fungus spreads into a healthy tree through its roots, traveling from an infected tree to another where crossed roots are grafted and growing together (not by means of mycorrhizal partnerships). The inoculum invades the living cambium of the tree, rising no more than a meter (3 feet) above the ground, but early symptoms of infection appear all the way up in the tree's crown, as the tree begins to appear stunted and yellow. Within a year of infestation, the tree's cones begin to drop prematurely, meaning that its reproductive years are all but over.

When the invader is well established, the bark of the lower trunk seems perpetually wet, darkened, and water stained, as though the tree cannot get warm or dry, as indeed it cannot, since the fungus has clogged up its xylem and phloem channels and prevented the tree from moving food and water. The rot spreads, and when it insinuates itself into the root, the tree's wood turns to pulp and the rings in its lower trunk begin to laminate, separating one from another like curved shales. Before long, the tree is dead, though it will remain standing for years as a snag. Devoid of needles, it makes an ideal spot for birds to rest and survey the surrounding territory for prey or predators. A tree that has lived for a thousand years will die in two or three. Deprived of its solid root hold in the ground, it can be blown down by a good wind.

Annosus root and butt rot are caused by *Heterobasidion annosum*, a fungus whose spores float through the air all year round and can invade a tree through wounds in its stem and roots—a branch fallen off, a gouged trunk caused by a falling neighbor, a woodpecker hole. Once inside, the fungus slowly reduces the tree's heartwood to a white, stringy mass surrounded by a spongelike shell. Eventually the trunk becomes hollow, its supply lines to its own roots cut off by the invader; the roots die; the tree falls.

Its boughs could already be infected by Douglas-fir needle blight, caused by the fungus *Rhabdocline pseudotsugae*, which first shows up as tiny yellow spots on the underside of the tree's new spring needles. Nothing happens that year, but over the winter the yellow spots darken to a deep reddish brown as the fungal spores insinuate their tiny hyphae through the needles' stomata and steal their winter juices. Soon all the tree's needles but the newest ones drop off, and the same ominous yellow spots appear on the new ones. By the end of the summer they, too, will have abscised and fallen to the ground. An infested tree is a dead tree.

The affliction most evident to an observer is the dwarf mistletoe *Arceuthobium douglasii*, which grows only on Douglas-firs. It is one of a thousand species related to the familiar green parasite under which, in a European tradition, some people like to kiss at Christmas. Mistletoe berries are much loved by birds, which help to disperse the seeds in their feces. (The word *mistletoe* comes from the German *mist*, meaning "dung," and the Old English *tan*, or "twig"; a bird deposits its dung on the twig, and in a year or two, Merry Christmas.) The eastern variety, *Phoradendron flavescens*, is found throughout southern New England in dense bunches up to a meter (3 feet) across; dwarf mistletoe, as its name implies, rarely gets bigger than 2 or 3 centimeters (about an inch). It is a total parasite, having no chlorophyll of its own. The male and female plants exist separately; in spring the male plant exudes spores from which the female plant grows on the same tree. In the fall the female produces seeds in dark-brown or purplish berries, which, when ripe, she can propel by means of a hidden spring to neighboring trees up to 15 meters (50 feet) away. The seed, encased in a sticky pulp, adheres to the bark of its host and, once it has germinated, insinuates its tiny haustoria, or food-absorbing outgrowths, into the moist phloem layer and begins to suck. The haustoria swell enormously thanks to water and nutrients stolen from the host, causing enlarged deformities in the weakened parts of the tree. A virus sets in, and the resulting ring of thin shoots—the male plant—weakens a tree even more; often, if a young tree is going to snap off during a violent windstorm, it will do so just above this apron of up-pointing mistletoe shoots. The result is sometimes called a witch's broomstick, since what is left looks suggestively like a broom stuck handle-first in the ground.

THE *G*RASS MAN

Douglas-fir mistletoe, like Douglas-fir itself, and Douglas aster, Douglas gentian, Douglas's brodiaea (aka bluedicks), Douglas's buckwheat, and Douglas's onion were all collected in 1825 by David Douglas on his first botanical expedition to the Pacific coast. He was known to the Natives of the Pacific coast as "the Grass Man." Although regarded suspiciously at first, he was soon declared quite harmless and left to his own devices. He had poor eyesight and was frequently observed dropping to his knees in a forest glade and exclaiming excitedly over nothing. Born in Perth, Scotland, in 1799, as a youth he had worked as gardener for Sir Robert Preston near Dumferline, in the Kingdom of Fife, where ornamental grasses are still the rage, and in 1820 he was apprenticed at the Glasgow Royal Botanical Gardens to William Jackson Hooker. Three years later he was engaged by the Horticultural Society of London as a collector and was sent to North America three times. On this trip, his second, after a dismal, eight-month voyage through rough seas, he descended from his ship at the mouth of the Columbia River. "With truth," he wrote in his journal, "I may count this one of the happy moments of my life."

Nothing had prepared him for the immensity of the forest in which he now found himself. He recorded his discovery of the sugar pine (*Pinus lambertiana*), one of the largest trees in the world. A fallen specimen was 75 meters (245 feet) in length and 17 meters (57 feet) around at the base. Forty-one meters (134 feet) from the ground, it was still 5 meters (17 feet) in circumference. To secure living cones, he eyed a standing specimen: "As it was impossible either to climb the tree or hew it down, I endeavoured to knock off the cones by firing at them with ball, when the report of my gun brought eight Indians, all of them painted with red earth, armed with bows, arrows, bone-tipped spears, and flint knives." Douglas coolly explained what he was after, and soon the eight men were helping him gather cones.

His encounter with Douglas-fir was less dramatic but equally memorable. "Tree remarkably tall," he wrote, "unusually straight, having the pyramid form peculiar to the *Abies* [Fir] tribe of Pines. The trees, which are interspersed in groups or standing solitary in dry upland, thin, gravelly soils or on rocky situations, are thickly clad to the very ground with wide-spreading pendent branches, and from the gigantic size which they attain in such places and from the compact habit uniformly preserved they form one of the most striking and truly graceful objects in Nature." Trees in the forest were even higher, but they were unclimbable, since their lowest branches were 42 meters (140 feet) above the ground. He measured a fallen specimen: "entire length, 227 feet [69 meters]; 48 feet [14.6 meters] in circumference 3 feet [1 meter] above the ground; 7½ feet [2.23 meters] in circumference 159 feet [48 meters] from the ground." Behind one of the Hudson's Bay Company buildings was a stump "which measures 48 feet [14.6 meters], 3 feet [1 meter] above the ground, without its bark. The tree was burned down," he observed, "to give place to a more useful vegetable, namely potatoes."

On his third and final trip, 1830 to 1833, he based himself in Fort Vancouver (now Vancouver, Washington). By this time his eyesight had deteriorated considerably. He had plants brought to him and himself carried to plants, mostly by canoe along the heavily indented coast. After two years he decided to return to England via Siberia and struck north along the Inside Passage with a guide and all his specimens and notebooks in a canoe. They made it to the Fraser River, but there his canoe overturned and he lost four hundred specimens and very nearly his life. After returning to Fort Vancouver, he decided to take the safe route home, by way of Hawaii. He remained in Hawaii for ten months and would have stayed longer, but on July 12, 1834, while on a walk to collect plants, he stumbled into an animal trap and was gored to death by an enraged boar. He was thirty-five years old. Of the ninety-two thousand species of plants then known to science, Douglas had discovered and collected seven thousand.

SNAGS AND SPOTTED *O*WLS

A tree is weak, as in exhausted, for a year after peak seed production. So much of its carbohydrate reserves are packed into the seeds that if two or three trees in a mycorrhizal assemblage produce the maximum number of seeds in the same year, the whole community is depleted. The starch larder gives out before new needles appear in the spring. A drought that summer, accompanied by excessive heat, a high rate of evaporation, and blasts of sunlight inhibiting photosynthesis, compounds the problems caused by poor needle renewal, slow bud growth, and low auxin production. Then if winter brings a prolonged period of cold, with temperatures below -10°C (14°F) for a week or more, the tree can be weakened beyond endurance. No single enemy kills a tree, but few trees can withstand a series of concentrated, simultaneous stresses on a variety of fronts over a number of years.

Bald eagle on a snag

Tree

It is 1867, the year the Mexican emperor Maximilian is assassinated; the year Russia sells Alaska to the United States for $7 million; the year Karl Marx publishes *Das Kapital;* the year the Red Shirts, under Giuseppe Garibaldi, make their second unsuccessful attempt to seize Rome; the year the Dominion of Canada is formed by the British North America Act. Despite our tree's arsenal of chemical defenses, it is no surprise when its needles turn a telltale orange in the spring. But most of the effective pathogen-toxic chemicals are produced by the flowering plants, the angiosperms, upstarts that evolved after root-rotting fungi and defoliating insects appeared on the evolutionary scene. In the evolutionary process, first came the gymnosperms, then insects and fungi that fed on gymnosperms, and then the angiosperms, which vastly outcompeted the gymnosperms because they manufactured secondary compounds that both attracted and repelled insects and fungi—they controlled their enemies rather than remaining at their mercy. An unfortunate coincidence of several stresses has weakened our tree's immune system, allowing insects and fungal pathogens to make it past the security checkpoints at the borders and overrun the capital. It has been handed its own Treaty of Nanjing. No tree dies of old age, and no tree lives forever.

Nitrogen is the main factor limiting a tree's growth; death is prolonged nitrogen deficiency. Nitrogen is also what an insect is after and what a fungus processes. So when a tree is under attack from insects or fungi or both, its first instinct is to protect its nitrogen. When a needle turns orange, the tree is abandoning any effort to save that needle by salvaging its nitrogen and sending it to another, so-far-unattacked part of the tree. This is admittedly a rearguard action, but a tree struggles as long as it has a living cell within it.

At some point, trying to save a single needle is a needless expense of energy. Old needles drop, and fewer new needles form. Insect larvae devour the buds; fungus spreads into the heartwood and travels down to the root. One of the last things our tree does before the fungus clogs its arteries is send its remaining secondary products, its chemical arsenal, down to its roots, out through the mycorrhizal fungi, and into the roots of neighboring trees, some of which are almost certainly its own offspring. In a poignant drama, our tree, having reached the point of death, gathers its remaining chemical weapons and donates them to the community, thereby giving its genetic future a slightly improved chance of fending off the invader that has spelled its own doom.

Death is part of a tree's cycle of life. A tree grows by turning living cambium into dead heartwood. Many organisms display similar dying/living cycles; in human embryos, for example, specific cells in growing limb buds are programmed to die to make the indentations that will become the spaces between digits, and cells in a tadpole's tail die to be reabsorbed into its metamorphosing body. Our tree's survival strategy is to fill the pores of its heartwood with secondary products to prevent it from rotting, but this tactic cannot go on forever; insects and even fungi evolve faster than trees do and build up ways to penetrate the chemical defenses. Cell walls are breached, systems drain, and one ring after another turns red with fungus and becomes a layer of wet pulp. Even at its most vigorous stage, only about 10 percent of a tree is alive. Death is a gradual lowering of that percentage.

Even when the tree is dead, however, its life is far from over. There is no definable moment of death, as there is with animals, when the last breath is expired or the heart stops beating or the brain loses oxygen. Even when our tree has ceased all metabolic activity, it does not fall. It remains standing as a snag. Its center is spongy in places, hollow in others, but there is plenty of sound wood in its periphery. A living tree can remain standing as long as 10 percent of its diameter is solid; a hollow tree with a diameter of 3.5 meters (11 feet) will remain upright if its trunk walls are only 15 centimeters (6 inches) thick. A snag requires even less sound wood because it has no needles and branches to catch the wind. In a windstorm, a snag is a ship with its sails furled. As such, it provides a safe haven for a number of birds, insects, and other animals. Pileated woodpeckers make huge, oval-shaped holes in the trunk; it is unclear whether they make the holes to look for ants or if they know that holes in dead trees eventually attract ants. Some of the holes are tenanted by nesting nuthatches. Others are used by flying squirrels as entryways into the tree's hollow interior, which explains why the stubs of the tree's former branches serve as perches for Cooper's hawks and northern spotted owls on constant lookout for their next meal.

Northern spotted owls (*Strix occidentalis caurina*) are medium sized, the males averaging 48 centimeters (19 inches) long and the females 42 centimeters (16½ inches) long. They are chocolate brown above and white below, with white spots on their head, neck, and wings; their throat and abdomen and the underparts of their tail are also barred brown. They appear to have dark rims around their eyes, as though from chronic lack of sleep. They do not migrate but live full-time in the old-growth forest by varying their diet from summer to winter. They have been known to prey on thirty species of mammals and twenty-three species of birds, as well as on snakes, crickets, beetles, and moths. In the summer, from just after dusk to about a half-hour before sunrise, they perch on snags and pick off flying squirrels that glide to the ground to dig up truffles; in winter they descend upon rabbits that venture out on top of the snow and on smaller rodents that frequent the tree's limbs and canopy mats. They often cache their prey in tree hollows, after decapitating them—the brain is a concentrated ball of nutrients.

In addition to perching on snags and caching food in them, northern spotted owls also nest in and forage in snags for cavity-dwelling prey. As a result, the owls are almost totally dependent on old-growth coniferous forests; 95 percent of their nesting sites are in forests older than two hundred years, and the other 5 percent are in second-growth stands adjacent to old growth. Their home ranges are huge—as large as 3,200 hectares (nearly 8,000 acres) per nesting pair in the northern forests, where game is less abundant. They nest in the hollows of lightning-struck trees or broken-off snags, and sometimes in the holes made by woodpeckers and vacated by flying squirrels; they kill the squirrels and then take over their homes. They also make use of abandoned northern goshawk nests or build their own nests in clumps of dwarf mistletoe, but they are not good at construction.

The owls return to the same nest year after year until it falls apart and then find another. The female lays two or three eggs in early April, each egg three days apart, and does all the incubating and brooding while the male brings the food. Both parents protect the nest—ravens will steal the eggs, and goshawks will take the nestlings. The owls have no enemies other than nest parasites. Some owls have been known to carry live snakes up to their nests to eat parasites and to discourage ravens and hawks. The nestlings fledge in six weeks and by October are ready to disperse to find their own ranges, often up to 200 kilometers (125 miles) from the parental nest, which is why extensive, connected tracts of old-growth forest are crucial to their survival. They seldom hunt in open or burned areas, and they frequent young forests only when forced to by lack of their preferred habitat. Many yearling spotted owls starve to death during their first winter.

Spotted owls were described and named in 1860 by John Xántus de Vesey, a Hungarian immigrant who had joined the U.S. Army in 1850 and was stationed at Cape San Lucas, in southern California, as part of the army's mandated exploration and mapping of the American West. De Vesey worked as a tidal observer while collecting specimens for the Smithsonian Institution, which had opened in 1856. At that time the spotted owl's range stretched all the way into Mexico. De Vesey found the bird unnaturally tame; he could walk up to one, he reported, without startling it into flight, an ominous trait since the same behavior had been characteristic of the dodo and the great auk. By the time he gave the world its first spotted owl, the forces of the species' extirpation were already invading the forest.

By the mid-1970s, northern spotted owls were all but eliminated from their former ranges because of habitat loss—mostly from logging, but natural causes also played a part. A huge fire in 1888 destroyed 10,000 hectares (25,000 acres) of old-growth forest. The eruption of Mount St. Helens in 1980 flattened another 10,000 hectares, and a century fire in 1987 destroyed 40,000 hectares (100,000 acres) of prime spotted owl habitat. By that time, American wildlife biologists estimated their numbers to be in the hundreds—there are now only fourteen breeding pairs left

Spotted owl with flying squirrel

in Canada, all of them in British Columbia—and urged the U.S. Forest Service, principally charged with ensuring a steady supply of trees to the lumber markets, to set aside protected old-growth areas around known spotted owl habitat. Some areas were set aside, amid protests from the industry, but not enough: less than 4 percent of the total timber base and less than half of what the owl needs to survive.

Human needs, amplified by industrial technology, are not compatible with the requirements of other species. Even though spotted owls have been greatly reduced in British Columbia, logging continues in the old-growth forest where the last birds remain. Current projections suggest that the northern spotted owl will be extinct long before the end of this century. And since it is an indicator species, when the spotted owl is gone we will know that the old-growth forest that sustains it and many other species has virtually disappeared as well.

Big Trees

It began as a circus act. In 1854, an ex–gold miner named George Gale stripped a giant sequoia of its bark to a height of 30 meters (100 feet) and sent it east in pieces to P. T. Barnum, who had it stitched back together and put on display as part of his Greatest Show on Earth. Few easterners believed that such a huge tree—it was 27 meters (90 feet) around at its base—existed in nature; it was the King Kong of its day. Similar skepticism greeted another such display at the Crystal Palace in England, stripped from a still-standing tree in North Calaveras Grove, east of San Francisco. According to historian Simon Schama, the trees were viewed as monstrosities, "botanical freak shows," as he writes in *Landscape and Memory*.

In California, the living trees attracted more positive attention. Parties of tourists, called pilgrims, were transported to Calaveras Grove to view the stand of Big Trees that had been discovered there; many were cut down, not only for the vast amount of lumber each tree provided—it took three weeks for a team of five men to fall and buck a single tree—but also so that their corpses could serve as a kind of natural amusement park. "A two-lane bowling alley was built (complete with protecting shed) along a planed-down surface of a trunk," Schama writes, "and the stump of a felled sequoia was made into a dance floor." On the 4th of July, 1855, thirty-two people danced four sets of cotillion on a single stump.

The Big Trees became something of a national monument, a symbol, writes Schama, "embodying both national magnitude and spiritual redemption." The United States was developing a continental consciousness, a sense that the nation stretched not only from coast to coast but also from the future back to the beginning of time. The trees connected the present with the barely imaginable past. Horace Greeley, who had gone west as a young man and enjoined other young men to follow him, marveled at the Big Trees' immense age. They dated, he wrote, from a time "when David danced before the Ark; when Theseus ruled Athens; when Aeneas fled from the burning wreck of Troy." Even the younger trees, others observed, had been growing in biblical times; in fact, they were contemporaries of Christ himself. "What lengths of days are here!" wrote the western correspondent for the Boston *Daily Advertiser* of a certain tree in 1869: "His years are the years of the Christian era; perhaps in the hour when the angels saw the Star of Bethlehem standing in the East, this germ broke through the tender sod and came out into the air of the Upper World."

So potent a rejuvenation of the American Dream were these trees that Abraham Lincoln, in the midst of the Civil War that most threatened that dream, signed the papers in 1864 that set aside Yosemite as America's first national park, largely at the urging of John Muir, who referred to the sequoia grove as "the Holy of Holies." The act spared a vast old-growth forest but also underscored the need for such an area to be protected from logging.

Farther north, where our tree now stands as a snag, the lure was not so much religious as it was economic. Douglas-fir are less imposing and easier to cut down than giant sequoias, and their wood is better. In 1847, tests conducted in England determined that spars made from Douglas-fir were superior to those made from white pine or Baltic spruce, which the British navy had been using until then. The Admiralty promptly announced that it would pay £45 for a single, 62-foot (19-meter) Douglas-fir spar 20 inches (50 centimeters) in diameter, and £100 for a 74-footer (22.5 meters) 23 inches (58 centimeters) in diameter, which made trade in Douglas-fir spars more lucrative than opium.

Captain William Brotchie, aboard the *Albion,* sailed into the Strait of Juan de Fuca, anchored off New Dungeness, and had his crew cut down £3,000 worth of spars, unfortunately from trees on American, not Canadian, soil. When his ship and its cargo were impounded by U.S. Customs, Brotchie relocated to Vancouver Island and hired Native laborers to cut 107 new spars. Without a ship, however, he had to leave them where they were stacked. Brotchie took a job as harbormaster for Vancouver Island, and by the time he died in 1859, a growing number of entrepreneurs had fully realized the value of Douglas-fir timber. During the next decade, 60 million board feet (about 1.5 million cubic meters) of lumber, as well as shingles, laths, pickets, and 3,500 spars, were shipped from Victoria to England, Australia, and Latin America. Passengers on the first CPR train that pulled into the thriving sawmill city of Vancouver on May 23, 1887, found the streets decorated with great arches of evergreen boughs, as though some pre-Christian festival were in progress, perhaps to appease the tree gods. By that time sixty-two sawmills were in operation within sight of the city; the train made the 137-hour return trip to Montreal with a load of lumber.

A SINGLE Organism

The idea of a forest as "a community of trees" was first proposed by the Russian geographer Georgy Fedorovich Morozov, who, although almost totally unknown in the West, was the founding spirit of modern ecology. Morozov was born in 1867 in St. Petersburg. During his military service he was sent to Latvia, where he met and fell in love with the young revolutionist Olga Zandrok, who encouraged him to devote himself to the agricultural sciences so that his knowledge would benefit the people. Morozov chose forestry, and upon his return to St. Petersburg with Zandrok he enrolled at the university and studied not only forestry but also zoology and anatomy; he was interested in the mutual relationship between an organism's form and its function. An ardent Darwinist, he came to appreciate nature as a complex web of interrelationships and the evolution of plant species as a function of a whole host of influences, including soil type, climate, insects, plant communities, and human activities.

After studying forest management in Germany and Switzerland in 1896, Morozov returned to Russia and became professor of forestry at St. Petersburg University, where he remained until 1917. His teachings and papers established forest management as a legitimate subdiscipline of botany. A forest, he wrote in *The Forest as a Plant Society* in 1913, "is a single, complex organism with regular interconnections among its parts and, like every other organism, distinguished by a definite stability." If that stability is altered or destroyed by human causes or climate change (in 1891 he had witnessed the disastrous effect of a major drought on the pine forest in the Voronezh district), the forest suffers, in some cases irretrievably—and not only the forest but also the numerous creatures that form the forest community, including humans. Morozov believed that "a forest is not simply an accumulation of trees, but is itself a society, a community of trees that mutually influence each other, thus giving rise to a whole series of new phenomena that are not the properties of trees alone." Plants adapt not only to new climates and soil conditions, he stated, but also to each other, as well as to the specific animals, insects, birds, and bacteria that surround them. The forest is an intricate, delicately balanced house of cards from which no one card can be pulled without bringing the entire structure crashing down around our heads.

In 1918, suffering from a serious nervous disorder (perhaps a euphemism for lack of enthusiasm for the October Revolution of 1917), Morozov was forced to retire from his post and move to the milder climate of the Crimea, where he observed the rapid and senseless destruction of the Russian forest. He died two years later, at the age of fifty-three.

As the fierceness of the debate over the spotted owl has shown, Morozov's message—that we cannot pluck one organism out of the forest community without affecting every other member of it, including humans—failed to reach the ears of the West Coast lumber barons. Douglas-fir is now the most important timber species in North America; billions of board feet of lumber are cut and shipped annually. The spotted owl is only one species affected by timber cutting. As a forest manager, Morozov understood downward spirals: in one possible scenario, removing old-growth trees threatens to extirpate the spotted owl, which could mean an increase in flying squirrels, which might cause a shortage of the squirrels' principal food item—truffles—which would in turn reduce the amount of mycorrhizal fungi available to new trees, which could result in a less healthy, less economically viable forest. The spotted owl is thus a symbol of forest health; a threat to the owl is a threat to the entire system. At an early hearing convened by the Washington Wildlife Commission to decide whether or not to declare the spotted owl an endangered species, a member of the National Rifle Association stated that "this is not a spotted owl situation, this is an old-growth situation." He was only half right: forest ecology is not an either-or proposition; it is a spotted owl situation *and* an old-growth issue. It is also a human issue. And it is a planetary issue.

As biologist E.O. Wilson has observed, "the loss of forests during the past half-century is one of the most profound environmental changes in the history of the planet." It is a loss that has been going on since human beings invented stone tools. Two thousand years ago, virtually every landmass was forested. Roman legions felled the forests of southern France so that their Celtic enemies could not sneak up on them. By 1750, France was only 37 percent wooded; 25 million hectares (60 million acres) of forest had been destroyed in nine decades. By 1860, the loss was 33 million hectares (80 million acres) and was increasing at the rate of 42,000 hectares (over 100,000 acres) per year. Great Britain was even more denuded. When David Douglas was wandering open-mouthed through the Douglas-fir forest, the British Isles were less than 5 percent forested—there was less than 40 square meters (a tenth of an acre) of forest per person; the only thing that kept Britain in energy was its enormous coal deposits, which were themselves the remnants of ancient fern forests. Norway, by comparison, was 66 percent forested at that time, with an average of 10 hectares (25 acres) for each citizen. England, no less than the Crimea, had cut down all its trees, and it was plantations of Douglas-fir seedlings from North America that revived its vanished forest industry.

The cutting has been going on worldwide ever since and has escalated exponentially in recent decades. According to the United Nations, since 1980 (when the alarm was sounded for the spotted owl) the world's forests have been reduced at the rate of 1 percent per year. The temperate Douglas-fir forest of western North America is now less than 20 percent of its original, precontact size, and most of what remains consists of isolated old-growth pockets, "habitat islands," as Wilson calls them. No wildlife corridors connect them, and as the spotted owl situation suggests, biodiversity is already declining within them. Even these isolated pockets are slated for cutting. Wilson notes that an ecosystem can tolerate the loss of 90 percent of its area and still allow half of its biodiversity to hang on—to an untrained or biased observer, everything might appear to be all right. The removal of any more than that 90 percent of an area, however, "can wipe out the remaining half in one stroke." And it takes very little to cross that critical threshold. "In a nightmare scenario," writes Wilson, "battalions of loggers armed with bulldozers and chainsaws could wipe these habitats off the face of Earth in a few months."

To be fair to forestry companies, an old-growth Douglas-fir forest seems bent on destroying itself. It is not a finished forest but a community in transition. Eventually, all the Douglas-firs in the uplands forest will have grown too big to sustain themselves or will be killed by insects or fungi and will give way to the trees waiting patiently in the understory, the western hemlocks and western redcedars, to take over and become a climax forest. In this way of looking at a forest one may ask, why shouldn't lumbermen assist in this natural process by taking out the big trees while they are still worth something? Taking this reasoning further, the old trees can be replaced by new, improved Douglas-fir seedlings, genetically modified to have less troublesome lignin, grow faster, and be resistant to an array of pests and diseases. That, at least, is how biotechnologists and the forest industry paint the picture.

In a natural habitat, when a spotted owl loses its home range to a hemlock-redcedar climax forest, it can relocate to another old-growth Douglas-fir locale. If all the trees surrounding its habitat island have been cut down, however, there is nowhere else to go. A plantation of big trees does not constitute an old-growth forest. A natural climax forest embraces trees of all ages, from seedlings to snags, includes deadfall and leaf litter on the forest floor, and supports salmon populations and all their predators. A reforestation project is a monocultural farm; it is the opposite of biodiversity. As a 1984 study conducted by the Society of American Foresters recognized, "there is no evidence that old-growth conditions can be reproduced silviculturally. In fact the question is essentially moot, as it would take two hundred years or more to find an answer." The spotted owl does not have two hundred years.

The snag has become a favorite resting place for a cougar. It is an aging male; he spends much of the day dozing at the snag's base, hunting in the late afternoon and slipping down to the stream for a quiet drink in the evening. Because of the nature of the old-growth forest, there are not many large predatory mammals about. Black bears and grizzlies are few and far between—an adult male grizzly has a home range of more than 1,500 square kilometers (580 square miles). The early settlers, like the Salish before them, stayed close to the coast, on the margin, dependent on the sea as much as on the land. When their settlements expanded, however, and women and children joined the men, cougars began to descend from the mountains to pick off the domestic dogs and cats the settlers' families brought with them. Suddenly, like the monster in *Beowulf,* a powerful predator that few people had ever seen had become a nightly visitor.

Cougars (*Felis concolor*) are large cats, males reaching up to 2.7 meters long (9 feet), including the tail. The average weight of an adult male is around 80 kilograms (180 pounds), although Theodore Roosevelt shot one that weighed 100 kilos (220 pounds), and the largest recorded animal, killed in Arizona in 1917, weighed 125 kilos (276 pounds). They are nocturnal, they do not hibernate, and in the forest they hunt from trees. Also known as mountain lions, pumas (an Incan word), panthers (in the south), painters, and catamounts (in the east), they wait on the lower limbs and drop onto whatever passes beneath, whether deer, elk, or human, then sink their canines into the victim's neck between the fourth and fifth cervical vertebrae, killing it instantly. If hunting in open terrain, they stalk their prey from behind, then

Cougar and uprooted tree

make a short, intensely powerful run at it, hitting it with their shoulder and knocking it to the ground. Their high-pitched cries at night during mating season—which can be any time of the year—sound like those of a woman being murdered with a slow-acting poison. They fill the forest, animating the darkness with unimaginable terrors. Canadian nature writer R.D. Lawrence, who once made his living hunting cougars, refers to the animal as the "ghost walker." He describes it as a highly evolved hunter, "silent and cautious as a rule, but exceptionally noisy when moved to utter its fearful cries of love or rage." As it pads through the forest, "it makes but the merest whisper of sound, lithe and graceful and perhaps more alert than any other North American predator."

The female delivers three or four kittens, usually in the spring but sometimes as late as August, and the two that will survive to adulthood stay with her for two full years, learning to hunt. They don't mate until their third year; a male and female will travel together for a week or so until the mating is complete, then separate to establish their own home ranges, which can be up to 800 square kilometers (300 square miles) and shift in size and location from season to season, as game availability fluctuates. Because an adult cougar kills up to sixty deer-sized ungulates a year, it requires a herd of up to seven hundred prey animals to support it, which explains its huge home range. (Ecologist Tom Reimchen observes that in nature a predator never takes more than 6 percent of its prey species; humans, however, think it is possible to "manage" wild species like salmon, deer, or ducks so that they can take 80 or 90 percent and still retain their numbers.) If game is plentiful, as it still is around our tree, the cat may kill often and eat only the liver, kidneys, and intestines of its prey; in some instances it will simply make a small incision in the animal's jugular and take nothing but the blood.

LIFE IN DEATH

Our tree stands as a snag for sixty-two years, home to a succession of creatures besides the cougar: woodpeckers, one flammulated owl, flying squirrels, chipmunks, spotted bats, chickadees, and nuthatches. Eventually, as fungi continue their relentless spread throughout the tree, they soften the root's hold on the dead stem, and the tree's attachment to the ground becomes more a matter of poise than anchorage. In the fall of 1929, a storm blowing up from the now-populous coast worries the snag back and forth like a tongue with a loose tooth, as buffets of rain-laden wind rise up the ridge and bounce among the living trees. Without its bark the snag soaks up water, more on the windward side, and after a while a low, scraping groan rises from its base, where gravelly soil attached to the tree's deeper roots shears against the unmoving ground. Most of the tree's denizens have scurried from their nests despite the rain to seek new shelter in sounder snags. After several nights of rocking, the snag is unable to regain its equilibrium and falls into the wind, crashing among its neighbors, guided away from their trunks by their downward-sloping boughs until, 30 meters (100 feet) from the forest floor, the branches give way and the heavy snag drops freely into a low cushion of young hemlocks, several of which it takes down with it. No one hears it fall.

One of its limbs cracks and falls into the nearby stream, where it tumbles and twists with the current until, at a sharp bend where the water curves off, it becomes ensnared on the bank. There the branch will become partly buried in silt and provide cover for trout as well as food for a variety of insects. Other limbs scatter over the forest floor, adding their nitrogen-rich lichen to the soil.

Because the tree was a snag, its absence has left no hole in the canopy, and as a fallen log lying in deep shade it is quickly covered by mosses and fungi, which bring it to the attention of a pair of Pacific dampwood termites (*Zootermopsis angusticollis*). A winged female, or alate, lands beside the deadfall, followed by a similarly winged male. Both termites are light brown, almost translucent, about 10 millimeters (three-eighths of an inch) in length, with darker brown, heavily veined wings that bore them from their separate natal colonies in another part of the forest. When they land, their wings drop off, and together they excavate a shallow chamber in the side of the fallen snag, enter the chamber, seal it up from within, and mate.

Two weeks later, the female deposits twelve elongated eggs in the chamber, a meager clutch compared with the thirty thousand eggs per day laid by some African termites, but enough to begin a colony. The immatures will be of two castes, reproductives and soldiers, and will perform all of the work of the colony, which is mainly to excavate an intricate tunnel system throughout the snag and to bring food back to the queen and king. The following spring, the reproductives will deposit eggs in remote parts of the colony, the queen will deposit another clutch of twelve eggs, and this process will continue until the colony contains four thousand individuals. All the members of a colony are thus related; the overall colony is divided up into smaller family groups. The soldiers keep carpenter ants and other termites out of the colony's galleries, using their huge heads and powerful, toothed mandibles to block passageways and cut unwanted intruders in half at the waist.

Nurse log

Termites are social detritivores; they reduce the amount of rotting wood on the forest floor by speeding up its decomposition, thereby adding nutrients to the soil as quickly as possible. They swallow wood fiber, but they cannot digest it. They carry a population of microorganisms in their guts that break down cellulose and produce by-products, some of which the termites ingest and others, such as methane gas, they expel. When termites molt, shedding their tough exoskeletons in order to grow, they shed their guts as well as their skin and so must eat the fecal matter of their fellow colonists to replenish their supply of bacteria. They groom one another with their tongues and in so doing ingest spores of fungi that also live in their guts and help feed their bacterial symbionts. In the tropics, where termites create vast colonies of up to ten thousand individuals per square meter (10 square feet) of soil, they are the most dominant organism on the ground; their biomass exceeds that of all vertebrates in the same area. Anteaters know what they're doing. In the Pacific Northwest termites are not that dominant, but they are important. Up to one-third of all the deadwood on the forest floor is returned to soil by the action of termites. Just as important is the role that their intricate galleries perform as ready-made pathways for fungal spores and the roots of colonizing plants that arrive to take advantage of the softening wood of the decaying log.

SEVEN HUNDRED YEARS after its emergence as a young seedling, our tree is lying on the damp forest floor, a fallen giant now shrouded by its former understory rivals. It is decaying. In nature, death and decay support new life. The tree's wood has been invaded by dampwood termites and carpenter ants, by mites and springtails, by decomposing fungi and bacteria. Its armor of wood is riddled with holes. Very little light falls on it. It is, essentially, a deposit of slowly composting soil that will remain a discernible hump on the ground for hundreds of years. Cloaked by a thick layer of moss and ferns, the outline of our tree's carcass remains visible on the ground like a body beneath a blanket. One September, a light sprinkling of winged seeds will fall on it. Some will have fallen from the Douglas-firs still towering above, but most will be western hemlock seeds. The Douglas-fir seeds will not take root on our log, as they require sunlight and prefer mineral soil, such as the gravel beds our tree originally colonized after the century fire cleared the understory. But hemlock seeds thrive in rich, shaded, organic soil, and that is what our tree's interior will have become. In the spring, the young hemlocks' stringy roots will work their way down through the termite and ant holes into our tree's bole, where they will encounter the mycorrhizal fungi introduced on the backs of termites, and they will flourish and grow. Our log will have become a nurse for its rival species. Eventually, the new trees' exposed roots will straddle their nurse and enter the ground. When our tree finally dissolves into soil, there will be a long, almost perfectly straight row of western hemlocks in the forest, each tree perched on mounds formed by their own roots and the remains of our tree. The mounds will be covered by detritus, leaves from old vine maples, and the middens of Douglas squirrels, and will be shared by sword ferns, which will shelter salamanders watching for springtails.

Two human beings, walking through the dense forest, will see the straight line of hemlocks, and one of them will make the observation that there must have been a nurse log there at one time.

They will not know that the nurse log was once a giant Douglas-fir, born the year that Edward I became king of England, fallen the year of the great Wall Street Crash, but they will feel an unaccustomed oneness with the Earth just the same. They will take that feeling home, and it will sustain them.

SELECTED
REFERENCES

Allen, George S., and John N. Owens. *The Life History of Douglas Fir*. Ottawa: Environment Canada Forestry Service, 1972.

Altman, Nathaniel. *Sacred Trees*. San Francisco: Sierra Club Books, 1994.

Aubry, Keith B., et al., eds. *Wildlife and Vegetation of Unmanaged Douglas-Fir Forests*. Portland: United States Department of Agriculture, Forest Service, 1991.

Bonnicksen, Thomas M. *America's Ancient Forests: From the Ice Age to the Age of Discovery*. New York: John Wiley and Sons, 2000.

Brodd, Irwin M., Sylvia Duran Sharnoff, and Stephen Sharnoff. *Lichens of North America*. New Haven, CT: Yale University Press, 2001.

Clark, Lewis J. *Wild Flowers of the Pacific Northwest*. Madeira Park, BC: Harbour Publishing, 1998.

Drengson, Alan Rike, and Duncan MacDonald Taylor, eds. *Ecoforestry: The Art and Science of Sustainable Forest Use*. Gabriola Island, BC: New Society Publishers, 1997.

Ervin, Keith. *Fragile Majesty: The Battle for North America's Last Great Forest*. Seattle: Mountaineers, 1989.

Forsyth, Adrian. *A Natural History of Sex: The Ecology and Evolution of Sexual Behavior*. New York: Charles Scribner's Sons, 1986.

Tree

Fowles, John, and Frank Horvat. *The Tree*. Don Mills, ON: Collins Publishers, 1979.

Heinrich, Bernd. *The Trees in My Forest*. New York: HarperCollins Publishers, 1997.

Hölldobler, Bert, and Edward O. Wilson. *Journey to the Ants: A Story of Scientific Exploration*. Cambridge, MA: Belknap Press of Harvard University, 1994.

Huxley, Anthony. *Plant and Planet*. London: Allen Lane, 1974. New enlarged edition, Harmondsworth: Penguin Books, 1987.

Kendrick, Bryce. *The Fifth Kingdom*. 3rd ed. Newburyport, MA: Focus Publishing, 2001.

Lawrence, R.D. *A Shriek in the Forest Night: Wilderness Encounters*. Toronto: Stoddart Publishing Co., 1996.

Luoma, John R. *The Hidden Forest: The Biography of an Ecosystem*. New York: Henry Holt and Company, 1999.

Marsh, George Perkins. *Man and Nature: Or, Physical Geography as Modified by Human Action*. Cambridge, MA: Harvard University Press, 1864.

Maser, Chris. *Forest Primeval: The Natural History of an Ancient Forest*. Toronto: Stoddart Publishing Co., 1989.

———. *The Redesigned Forest*. Toronto: Stoddart Publishing Co., 1990.

Muir, John. *Wilderness Essays*. Salt Lake City: Peregrine Smith Books, 1980.

Pakenham, Thomas. *Meetings with Remarkable Trees*. London: Weidenfeld and Nicolson, 1996.

Platt, Rutherford. *The Great American Forest*. Englewood Cliffs, NJ: Prentice-Hall, 1965.

Savage, Candace. *Bird Brains: The Intelligence of Crows, Ravens, Magpies and Jays*. Vancouver: Greystone Books, 1995.

Schama, Simon. *Landscape and Memory*. New York: Alfred A. Knopf, 1995.

Taylor, Thomas M.C. *Pacific Northwest Ferns and Their Allies*. Toronto: University of Toronto Press, 1970.

Thomas, Peter. *Trees: Their Natural History*. Cambridge: Cambridge University Press, 2000.